W9-CRF-346

South Bay Bike Trails

*Road and Mountain Bicycle Rides
through Santa Clara and Santa Cruz Counties*

by
Conrad J. Boisvert

Penngrove Publications
*50 Crest Way
Penngrove, CA 94951
(707) 795-8911*

To my late father, Conrad, Sr.,
who gave me a running start.

Library of Congress Catalog Card Number 90-62590
International Standard Book Number 0-9621694-2-0

Cover photograph by Jeff Dooley
Taken on West Cliff Drive in Santa Cruz.
Cyclists: Conrad Boisvert and Jana Cushman

Printed in the United States of America
Lithocraft, Inc.
947 Piner Place
Santa Rosa, California

First printing, September 1990

$\mathcal{P}$enngrove Publications
50 Crest Way
Penngrove, CA 94951
(707) 795-8911

TABLE OF CONTENTS

Explore the South Bay by Bike! 5
Regions of the South Bay 6
San Francisco South Bay Area 7
How to Use This Book 8
Rides
Santa Clara Valley: East Foothills 10
    1. San Felipe Valley 11
    2. New Almaden and Hicks Road Hill Climb 14
    3. Coyote Creek Bike Path 17
    4. Quimby Road Loop 20
    5. Grant Ranch County Park 23
    6. Alum Rock Park 27
Santa Clara Valley: West Foothills 30
    7. Saratoga and Stevens Canyon Back Roads 31
    8. Los Gatos, Villa Montalvo, and Saratoga 34
    9. Los Gatos Creek Trail 37
    10. Sierra Azul Open Space Preserve 41
    11. St. Joseph's Hill Open Space Preserve 46
Santa Cruz Area: Mountains and Beaches 50
    12. Mountain Charlie Road 51
    13. Santa Cruz and Capitola Beach Ride 55
    14. Along the Crest of Summit Road 58
    15. Eureka Canyon and Soquel Loop 62
    16. Forest of Nisene Marks State Park 66
West Santa Cruz Area: Mountains and Forests 72
    17. Empire Grade and Bonny Doon Loop 73
    18. Henry Cowell Redwoods State Park .78
    19. Big Basin Redwoods State Park 81
South County: Ranches and Farms 84
    20. Chesbro and Uvas Reservoirs 85
    21. Gilroy Hot Springs and Cañada Road 88
    22. Henry Coe State Park 91
    23. Mount Madonna Hill Climb 96
Watsonville Area: Orchards and Farms 99
    24. Corralitos and Green Valley Loop 100
    25. Rio Del Mar — Watsonville Loop 104
    26. Pajaro Valley and the Elkhorn Slough 107
    27. Corralitos and Summit Road Loop 110
Appendix
Rides by Ratings 114
Mountain Bike Rides 115
Bicycle Shops in the South Bay 116
Cycling Clubs in the South Bay 118
Annual Cycling Events 119
Fairs And Events in the South Bay 120
Points of Interest 121
California Bicycle Laws 123
Bicycling Tips 125

ACKNOWLEDGEMENTS

I am grateful to the many individuals who have encouraged and helped me to complete this book. I especially wish to acknowledge my mother, Helen, who always supported anything I chose to attempt.

My cycling buddies deserve mention for all the brainstorming we did and the suggestions they made. Among them, Sue Johnson, Tracie Mantia, Dennis Vanata and Holly Quittman rate a special note. Carl Hartshorn was invaluable for his computer help and for his general personal support. For personal encouragement, I thank Judy Johnson, Jana Cushman, my sons, Charles and Steve, and my lovely daughter, Judy.

Thanks also to my publisher, Phyllis Neumann, who knew what was required and inspired me with her enthusiasm and support, and to Jeff Dooley for his superb cover photograph. Linda Cardone's help with final editing was invaluable.

Finally, this book would have been impossible to complete without the help and friendly support of the many park rangers and employees of the California State Park System and the Santa Clara County Parks. In addition, I am thankful to Mark and Pam Silverstein for their knowledge of the Elkhorn Slough National Estuarine Research Center.

EXPLORE THE SOUTH BAY BY BIKE!

Northern California is unarguably the premier region in the world for bicycling. Few places can compare with its natural beauty, physical challenge, and diverse terrain. Long appreciated as a training ground for competitive cyclists, Northern California has become even more well known for its recreational cycling as a result of the recent explosion in the cycling phenomenon.

The San Francisco South Bay Area, although better known for its high-technology image, is a cyclist's paradise, when one escapes from the population centers and heads out into the surrounding countryside. The wide variety of roads and micro-climates offers the cyclist access to an unending series of adventures and relaxing relief from the pressures of the workplace and everyday life.

The South Bay is bounded on its eastern edge by the foothills beneath Mount Hamilton, as far north as San Jose, and as far south as Gilroy. To the west, the northern limit of this region is the community of Bonny Doon, along the coast, and at the southern limit are the town of Pajaro and the Elkhorn Slough.

The eastern and southeastern regions of the South Bay are dominated by ranches and farmlands. The hills can be quite challenging, although most rides in this book avoid the most extreme of the mountain climbs. The farmlands in and around Morgan Hill and Gilroy are quite often rich with the aromas of garlic and onions.

By contrast, the western part of the Santa Clara Valley is residential and is characterized by the fashionable homes of Los Gatos and Saratoga. On the other side of the Santa Cruz Mountains, heavy redwood forests line the sparsely populated western slope, leading to the beaches along the Pacific Ocean.

Heading south along the ocean brings you to the seaside resorts of Santa Cruz, Capitola, Rio Del Mar, and Pajaro Dunes. Beaches and state parks are numerous in this area.

Watsonville, Corralitos, and Pajaro further south are well-recognized for their contributions to agriculture, especially for artichokes, apples, and strawberries. The Elkhorn Slough, south of Pajaro, is one of the largest coastal wetlands and is an instrumental part of a string of wildlife refuges, protected by the state for use by the many migrating birds along the coast.

The rides in *South Bay Bike Trails* have been selected to appeal primarily to the recreational cyclist. The wide variety of regions and terrain described in this book will ensure that all levels of recreational riders will be able to use this book for years to come. Get on your bike and explore the San Francisco South Bay and share in the joy of cycling!

REGIONS OF THE SOUTH BAY

Santa Clara Valley: East Foothills

East of San Jose, in the foothills of the mountains below Mount Hamilton and Lick Observatory, the roads follow through areas occupied by ranches and pastureland and offer pastoral settings which can be a very pleasing escape from the sometimes hectic pace of the urban parts of the valley. The eastern hills of the Santa Clara Valley are often quite hot on summer days, since there is little shade to offer protection from the afternoon sun in the west.

Santa Clara Valley: West Foothills

At the western end of the Santa Clara Valley, the area is heavily wooded, in sharp contrast to the eastern end. This region is much cooler in the summer, as a result of both the abundant shade from the trees and the location on the eastern slope of the Santa Cruz Mountains. The towns of Saratoga and Los Gatos are focal points for cyclists in the area, with numerous restaurants, shops, and other diversions.

Santa Cruz Area: Mountains and Beaches

The beach environment of this region stands in stark contrast to the urban and suburban nature of the Santa Clara Valley, on the other side of the Santa Cruz Mountains. Being a traditional beach resort, there is usually a fair amount of traffic, especially during the summer months, but numerous bike lanes ensure an adequate level of safety.

West Santa Cruz Area: Mountains and Forests

This region extends from Santa Cruz up the coast to Bonny Doon and then inland to Big Basin. The roads are not heavily used by cars, but can be quite hilly. The area is dominated by forests and along the coast, beaches, and is a hidden jewel for cyclists.

South County: Ranch Country

This region, in the southernmost part of the South Bay, is characterized by an abundance of remote country roads with very little traffic. Unlike the other areas, however, there are few roadside restaurants or services, so it is usually a good idea to pack a snack. In addition, being inland results in a very dry environment and hot summer days.

Watsonville Area: Orchards and Farms

Although these rides are farther away from residential areas, and consequently may take a fair amount of driving to get to, they cover roads which carry very little traffic and are very pleasurable to ride. There are beaches in this area along the coast, but the best roads for cycling are inland, at the foothills of the mountains.

SAN FRANCISCO SOUTH BAY AREA

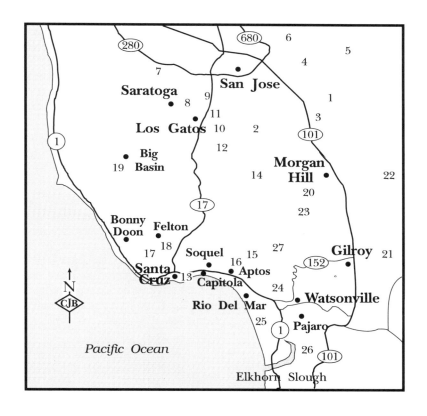

HOW TO USE THIS BOOK

Understanding the Ride Parameters

At the beginning of each ride description is a short list of ride parameters. These are intended to give you a brief summary of that particular ride and to permit you to sort through the rides for the one that best suits your needs.

Ride Rating — Reflects the overall difficulty of the ride, a simple judgement and classification into one of three possible categories: *Easy, Moderate,* or *Difficult.* This is usually a result of the distance and the total elevation gain of the ride, but can also be affected by the steepness of the hills.

Total Distance — Indicates the length of the ride, excluding any optional side trips which may be described in the ride.

Riding Time — Gives an indication of how much time to budget for the ride. Keep in mind, however, that this does not include extended stops for sightseeing, eating, and resting. The riding time usually assumes an average pace of about 8-10 miles/hour.

Total Elevation Gain — Combines the total elevation of all the hill climbing required. For example, climbing two hills, each with 500 feet of elevation gain, would result in 1,000 feet of total elevation gain.

Calories Burned — Approximates the total amount of energy burned. This is based upon an average calorie burn rate of around 300 calories/hour on a flat road at about 14 miles/hour and around 800 calories/hour on a hill climb with about an 8% grade, with a speed of approximately 4 miles/hour. Some variations will occur for individual differences or for external factors.

Type of Bike — Suggests road or mountain bike. Although a ride may have a stretch of dirt road, it may still be suitable for a road bike, if it is smooth and safe. Elaboration on this issue is usually found in the ride description.

Terrain

The general terrain and road conditions are briefly described to permit you to quickly determine if the ride is right for you. The best time of year for doing the ride is also provided to further enhance your riding enjoyment.

Ride Description

This section includes a general description of the ride, along with any interesting background or historical information for the area. Points of interest along the way are highlighted here as well. The general route to be followed is explained, although the details are saved for the *Ride*

Details and Mile Markers section. Extra side trip options or ride variations are explained in order to enhance your experience by adding to the basic ride.

Starting Point

The exact place to start the ride is described, along with detailed directions explaining how to get there. In general, rides are started at locations where free parking is readily available and where refreshments can be purchased for either before or after your ride. Typically the starting points are also easily recognizable places, simplifying the situation for a group of people meeting for a ride together.

Elevation Profile

The elevation profiles for each ride provide a detailed view of the required hill climbs. These not only preview the ride for you, but can be a useful reference to take with you on your ride, since they can help you anticipate terrain and prepare you for hills to be encountered.

Map

Each ride has a map associated with it indicating the route. Rides with more than one route are indicated with direction arrows on the map for each option. In general, however, the map is not necessary for following the route since detailed ride directions are included in the *Ride Details and Mile Markers* section.

Ride Details and Mile Markers

Directions for the route are described along with elapsed distances. You won't need a cycle computer for this, since the markers come at frequent intervals and you will quickly learn to estimate distances accurately enough. The markers indicate the required turns to take to follow the route, as well as point out special sights and features of the ride that you might otherwise miss.

Ride Options

Some rides have optional side trips which add to the basic ride. The features of these options are described, along with a brief explanation of directions to take and terrain to anticipate.

Ride Selections

Some rides offer several options. These are generally indicated with A, B, or C suffix designations to distinguish them. In most cases, they give the rider different levels of difficulty from which to choose. Separate *Ride Details and Mile Markers* for each variation ensures that there is no confusion about the ride directions and essentially results in each variation being treated as a separate ride.

Santa Clara Valley: East Foothills

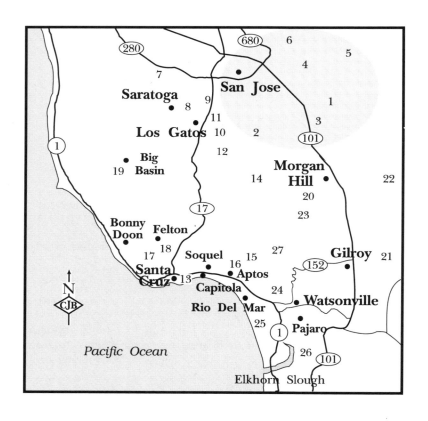

1

SAN JOSE
San Felipe Valley

Region: *Santa Clara Valley East*   **Ride Rating:** *Moderate*
Total Distance: *22 miles*   **Riding Time:** *2-3 hours*
Total Elevation Gain: *1300 feet*   **Calories Burned:** *700*
Type of Bike: *Road Bike*

Terrain

The roads are generally lightly traveled and well-paved, although they also lack a wide shoulder. This ride is good any time of year, however hot summer days may be somewhat uncomfortable.

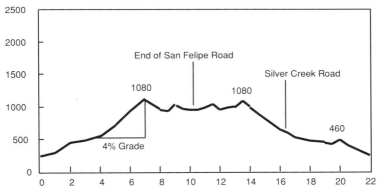

Ride Description

San Felipe Valley is just east of downtown San Jose, at the base of Mount Hamilton. The farms and ranches along the route offer many pastoral scenes for the cyclist. The apparent remoteness and peacefulness of the area stands in stark contrast to the bustling city, so near and yet seemingly so far away.

The ride starts in the Evergreen Valley section of East San Jose and proceeds southeast on San Felipe Road. Just past Evergreen Community College, the road changes its nature from residential/suburban to country. A steady climb takes you along the eucalyptus-lined road farther into the country. Frequent shade and a gentle grade combine to make this one of the best hill climbs for novice and low-intermediate riders.

After the first of two summits, a short downhill leads to the intersection with Metcalf Road, on the right and then, a bit later, with

Los Animas Road, also on the right. Another short climb leads to the other summit. About a mile beyond this summit is the end of the road, at the gate to the San Felipe Ranch in the heart of the San Felipe Valley. Turn back at this point and retrace your route until you get to Silver Creek Road, at which you will make a left turn.

Silver Creek Road goes uphill a short distance and then goes predominantly downhill, following the creek, to meet Yerba Buena Road. A right turn on Yerba Buena Road takes you back to San Felipe Road at Evergreen College. A left turn on San Felipe Road will return you to your starting point.

An alternate route of 10 miles is also provided for those not wishing to do the full ride. This route takes you out on San Felipe Road and brings you back on Silver Creek Road.

Starting Point
Start the ride at the intersection of Aborn Road, South White Road, and San Felipe Road. To get there, take the Capitol Expressway exit from Highway 101. Head east on Capitol Expressway to the intersection with Aborn Road, less than a mile away. Turn right on Aborn Road and drive about a mile to the starting point. There are several shopping centers at the corner where you may park your car.

Ride Details and Mile Markers
0.0 Proceed southeast on San Felipe Road. There is a bike lane on San Felipe Road.
1.4 Evergreen Valley Community College is on the left.
1.5 Cross Yerba Buena Road.
4.1 Silver Creek Road intersection is on the right. Turn right at this point for the short 10-mile ride option.
7.1 First summit — 1080 feet.
8.0 Metcalf Road intersection on the right.
8.5 Bear left to stay on San Felipe Road at the intersection with Los Animas Road, on the right.
9.0 Second summit — 1030 feet.
10.2 End of San Felipe Road at ranch entrance — go back.
11.4 Summit.
11.9 Bear right to stay on San Felipe Road.
13.4 Summit.
16.3 Turn left onto Silver Creek Road and climb a short distance.
19.6 Turn right onto Yerba Buena Road.
20.7 Turn left onto San Felipe Road.
22.2 Back at shopping center.

Shorter Option (10 miles)

At the 4.1 mile mark, turn right on Silver Creek Road, instead of continuing the climb on San Felipe. Continue along Silver Creek Road to the intersection with Yerba Buena Road, where you will turn right. Turn left on San Felipe to go back to where you started.

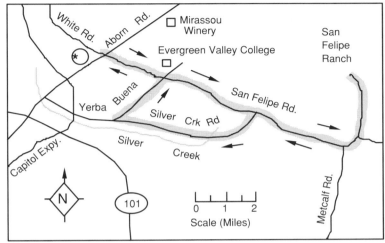

Ride 1

Picturesque bridge on San Felipe Road   Photo: Conrad J. Boisvert

2 SAN JOSE
New Almaden and Hicks Road Hill Climb

Region: *Santa Clara Valley East*
Total Distance: *20 Miles*
Total Elevation Gain: *1300 feet*
Type of Bike: *Road Bike*

Ride Rating: *Moderate*
Riding Time: *2-3 hours*
Calories Burned: *700*

Terrain

The majority of the ride is over country roads with one significant hill to climb. The ride is good anytime of year, although it is best in the spring, when the creeks are running and the hills are green.

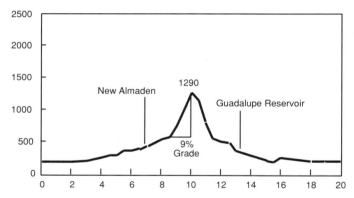

Ride Description

New Almaden was originally named for the town of Almaden in south-central Spain (about 100 miles south of Madrid) and has long been known for its rich, dark red earth which the native Indians of the area called "moketka." In 1824, Don Antonio Suñol began working a mining operation, thinking that the soil contained large quantities of silver. He abandoned these efforts when he concluded that no silver was present. Mining stopped completely until 1845, when Andres Castillero discovered that the red earth contained quicksilver, another name for the element, mercury.

Today, even though mining operations are no longer significant, New Almaden has retained its western flavor, and remains a throwback to previous times, despite its close proximity to San Jose's suburban sprawl.

This ride takes you from the Almaden Plaza Shopping Center to New Almaden along modern-day Almaden Expressway. After passing through New Almaden, you will ride by the Almaden Dam and Reservoir and then return to San Jose by going up and over the hill on Hicks Road, an elevation gain of about 800 feet. You will come down Hicks Road and pass by the Guadalupe Reservoir and Dam on the way back to the Almaden Plaza via Coleman Road and Almaden Expressway.

Starting Point

The ride starts from the Almaden Plaza Shopping Center at the intersection of Blossom Hill Road and Almaden Expressway in San Jose. To get there, take Highway 17 south toward Santa Cruz and get off at the Blossom Hill exit. Follow Blossom Hill Road east for about 5 miles to the intersection with Almaden Expressway. From Highway 101, south of San Jose, take the Blossom Hill Road exit and follow Blossom Hill Road west for about 4 miles to Almaden Expressway.

Ride Details and Mile Markers

0.0 Leave Almaden Plaza heading south on Almaden Expressway.

0.8 Cross Coleman Road.

1.8 Cross Redmond Road.

2.5 Cross Camden Avenue.

4.3 Turn right onto Almaden Road. (Almaden Expressway continues to the left.)

4.9 Mockingbird Hill Lane is on the right. If you proceed down this road, you will come to Almaden Quicksilver Park. Bikes are not permitted on the trails in the park, but you may wish to explore the park on foot.

6.8 Opry House is on the left. This is a New Almaden landmark. Melodramas and a rustic western-style bar are featured here.

7.0 Town of New Almaden. A small museum is on the left.

7.2 Another entrance to Almaden Quicksilver Park is on the right. California State Historic Landmark is on the left. Road changes name to become Alamitos Road.

8.9 Turn right to get on Hicks Road. Cross cattleguard immediately.

10.6 Summit — 1290 foot elevation. Loma Almaden Road is to the left (see description of the extra option on this route).

13.3 Guadalupe Reservoir and Dam are on the right.

14.4 Reynolds Road intersection is on the left.

15.5 Bear right at the Shannon Road intersection.

17.0 Turn right onto Camden Avenue and then make an immediate left onto Coleman Road.

19.0 Turn left on Almaden Expressway.

20.0 Back at the Almaden Plaza Shopping Center.

Extra Option on Loma Almaden Road (2 miles)

At the summit of Hicks Road is the intersection with Loma Almaden Road. If you take this optional side trip, you will climb about 900 feet over the 2-mile length of the road, with a portion of it very steep (about a 17% grade for one section about 0.2 mile long). You will reach a gate across the road where you can park your bike and walk along the trail off to the left for some spectacular views of the canyons below and Mt. Umunhum, ahead and off to the right. This is part of the Sierra Azul Open Space Preserve. Return down Loma Almaden Road to get back to Hicks Road, as there is no other exit.

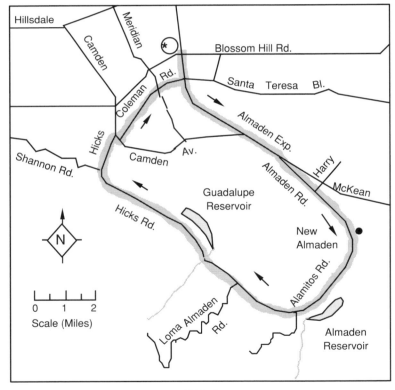

Ride 2

3 SAN JOSE
Coyote Creek Bike Path

Region: *Santa Clara Valley East*
Total Distance: *14 Miles*
Total Elevation Gain: *80 feet*
Type of Bike: *Road Bike*

Ride Rating: *Easy*
Riding Time: *1-2 hours*
Calories Burned: *300*

Terrain

The trail is paved, but rough in places. A road bike is fine, but the dirt trail on the levee at the far end of the bike path is better suited to the fat tires of mountain bikes. The ride is fairly flat and qualifies as one of the easiest rides in the South Bay.

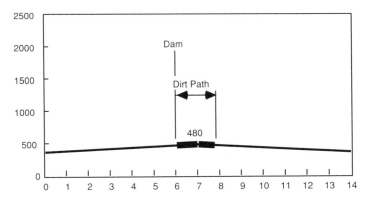

Ride Description

Hellyer Park is the start of the Coyote Creek Bike Path. This paved trail follows a leisurely route of about 7 miles along the tranquil Coyote Creek to the Coyote Percolation Basin, a small lake used for water skiing and fishing in the summer. The return is back along the same route, for a total distance of about 14 miles.

Hellyer Park is also home to the Hellyer Park velodrome, one of three bicycle race tracks in California. Originally built for the Pan American Games of 1962, it was not actually completed until 1963. More recently, it has been the site of the 1972 Olympic Bike Trials and numerous California State Championship Races. In the summer months, you can watch the Friday night races under the lights at the track, as well as frequent training rides by world-class racers in the mornings or evenings.

The bike path starts very near the velodrome. From the velodrome, as you head out toward the exit of the parking lot, there is a dirt path to the right of the road. This will lead you onto the bike path. From there, just follow it all the way to its end at the dam. You can go farther if you follow the rough dirt trail on the levee above the dam. This will take you to a boat launch used by water skiers in the summer months.

Starting Point

To get to Hellyer Park, go south on Highway 101 from San Jose. Get off at the Hellyer Avenue exit and go directly into the Hellyer Coyote County Park. Proceed straight ahead past the gate to the end of the road, where the velodrome is located.

Ride Details and Mile Markers

0.0   Leave the velodrome parking area the way you came in.

0.2   Just past the restroom on the right you will see a dirt trail off the road, to the right. This will lead you to the bike path.

0.7   Lake is on the left.

1.0   Bike path crosses under Highway 101.

3.2   Bike path seems to end at road. Cross over bridge on road, then get back on bike path on left side.

4.9   Cross directly over the road.

5.6   Bike path again goes under Highway 101.

6.1   Dam is on the left. Dirt path is to the right on the levee which may be rough.

6.6   End of dirt path at Monterey Highway. There is a dirt trail which continues on the left.

6.9   End of trail at boat launch area. Return the way you came.

7.7   Dam is on the right.

8.9   Cross over the road.

10.6   Turn right, go over the bridge, and turn left back on the trail.

13.8   Back at the velodrome.

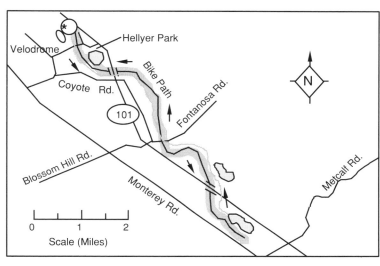

Ride 3

View of lake at the end of Coyote Creek Bike Path   Photo: Conrad J. Boisvert

4

SAN JOSE
Quimby Road Loop

Region: *Santa Clara Valley East*
Total Distance: *18 miles*
Total Elevation Gain: *2200 feet*
Type of Bike: *Road Bike*

Ride Rating: *Difficult*
Riding Time: *3 hours*
Calories Burned: *900*

Terrain

The majority of the ride is over country roads with one major hill climb. The ride is good any time of year, although it is best in the spring or the fall, when it is less likely to be hot.

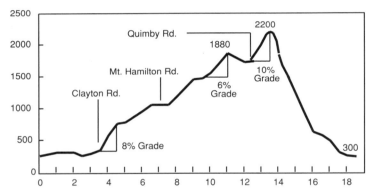

Ride Description

Mount Hamilton is one of the highest climbs available in the Bay Area and represents one of the top challenges for cyclists. This ride does not attempt to ascend the entire distance to the top, but instead, follows Clayton Road to Mount Hamilton Road, and then climbs only as far as Quimby Road, just before Joseph D. Grant County Park. The return on Quimby Road first climbs to the summit (elevation: 2260 feet) before descending steeply back into the valley.

The ride starts near the community of Evergreen on the east side of San Jose. The corner of Quimby Road and White Road provides ample parking and easy access to the loop, which begins at the intersection of Quimby Road and Ruby Road, just up the hill on Quimby.

Heading to the north on Ruby Road will take you through residential areas with a wide road and little traffic. This is generally a flat road and serves as a nice warm-up for the climb facing you on

Mount Hamilton. Shortly after Ruby Road merges with, and then becomes, Mt. Pleasant Road, the ride route turns on Marten Road to make the connection just up the hill at Clayton Road.

Clayton Road is an uphill climb and intersects Mount Hamilton Road part way up. This is a nice way to avoid the usually heavier traffic on Mount Hamilton Road. The route continues up Mount Hamilton Road and then down into the valley of the former Grant Ranch to the intersection with Quimby Road. Quimby Road has another climb to the peak of the ride, followed by the very steep and winding downhill back to White Road.

The roads are well paved, but lack a wide shoulder. This ride is good any time of year, although hot summer days should be avoided, since the major climbs are not shaded.

Starting Point

A good place to meet others and to park your car is at the intersection of White Road and Quimby Road, where several shopping centers exist. To get there, head south from San Jose on Highway 101. Take the Capitol Expressway exit and head east on Capitol Expressway to the intersection with Quimby Road. Turn right on Quimby Road to get to the corner of White Road.

Ride Details and Mile Markers

0.0   From the intersection of Quimby Road and White Road, go east on Quimby Road.

0.8   Turn left onto Ruby Road.

2.5   Ruby Road merges to become Mt. Pleasant Road.

3.0   Turn right onto Marten Road.

3.3   Turn right onto Clayton Road. Begin climb up winding road.

4.3   Orchards are on the right.

5.7   Intersection with Via De La Vista is on the right.

7.1   Very sharp right turn onto Mt. Hamilton Road.

10.5   Summit before Grant Ranch valley — 1880 feet.

12.3   Turn right onto Quimby Road — begin 10% climb.

13.2   Summit at Buckeye Ranch — 2264 feet.

13.3   Begin steep, winding descent — 14% grade downward.

16.4   Enter residential area.

17.5   Intersection with Ruby Road.

18.3   Intersection of Quimby Road and White Road.

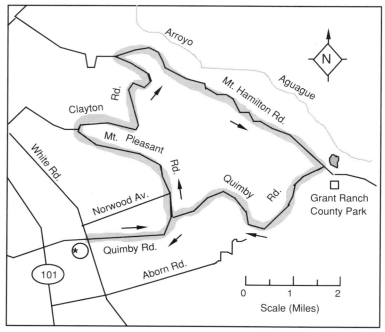

Ride 4

Ranch on Mount Hamilton Road

Photo: Conrad J. Boisvert

5 SAN JOSE
Grant Ranch County Park

Region: *Santa Clara Valley East*
Total Distance: *10 miles*
Total Elevation Gain: *1400 feet*
Type of Bike: *Mountain Bike*

Ride Rating: *Moderate*
Riding Time: *2 hours*
Calories Burned: *600*

Terrain

Grant Ranch County Park is primarily pastureland for livestock. It is generally open with very little shade, except for some stretches along the creeks. Constantly rolling, the terrain has many steep sections. The hot summer sun makes this ride best suited for spring and fall.

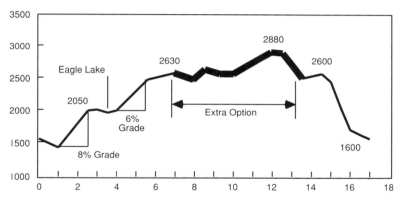

Ride Description

The Joseph D. Grant Ranch County Park was originally called the Rancho Cañada de Pala and was a part of a Mexican land grant given to Jose Jesus Bernal in 1839. The property changed hands several times until Joseph D. Grant inherited it from his father in the latter part of the nineteenth century.

After his death in 1942, his daughter, Josephine, became sole owner of the ranch. The property was left to the Menninger Foundation and the Save The Redwoods League upon her death in 1972. Finally, in 1975, Santa Clara County purchased the ranch for use in the county park system.

The park, encompassing some 9500 acres, is nestled in the foothills beneath majestic Mt. Hamilton and is populated with both livestock and wildlife. The land is rich in old oaks and is especially beautiful in the spring, when the meadows and slopes are alive with new growth. It is equally enjoyable at other times of year, when the colors take on a golden hue. Panoramic views are numerous, since the park is situated at a base elevation of about 1600 feet.

This mountain bike ride winds completely around the park and has an additional optional side trip, if you have some excess energy to burn.

Starting Point

To get to Grant Ranch County Park, proceed north from San Jose on Interstate Highway 680 and get off at the Alum Rock Avenue exit. Head east on Alum Rock Avenue for about 2 miles and turn right onto Mt. Hamilton Road. Grant Ranch County Park is about 8 miles up the road. Enter the park at the main entrance and continue all the way through and to the left side, where the visitor center and trailhead are located.

Ride Details and Mile Markers

0.0   Head east from the parking area. Go past two livestock gates to the Hotel Trail start.

0.3   Bear right on Lower Hotel Trail and begin descent.

1.0   Barn Trail intersection is on the right.

1.6   Livestock gate.

1.8   Go through the corral and the gate at the far side.

1.9   Steep uphill climb on loose gravel.

2.3   Trail intersection is on the left.

3.5   Eagle Lake is on the right — bear left and descend into the canyon. Begin Digger Pine Trail.

3.8   Cross stream and then go up a steep hill.

4.6   Turn left onto Bohnhoff Trail. This is a very steep climb.

4.9   Level section of trail.

5.5   Cross over Mt. Hamilton Road to get on Cañada de Pala Trail and climb immediately. If you are tired, you can return to your car on the road.

6.0   Yerba Buena Trail intersection of the left.

7.2   Gate.

7.3   Turn left onto Los Huecos Trail. Steep downhill. [Go straight ahead if you are doing the extra option.]

8.2   Gate.

8.9   Trail intersection is on the right.

9.1   Reservoir — turn left to stay on the trail.

9.4   Parking lot — go through and turn right onto Mt. Hamilton Road.

9.7   Turn left into park entrance.

10.2   End of ride at parking lot.

Extra Option to the Meadow (6 miles)

The extra option is in the northern side of the park. It covers about 6 miles as it leaves the main trail a completes a loop around a meadow on the Cañada de Pala and Pala Seca Trails.

At the 7.3 mile point, instead of turning left onto the Los Huecos Trail, continue straight ahead and stay on the Cañada de Pala Trail. It drops quickly and then climbs to the intersection with Pala Seca Trail where you will bear left in order to stay on Cañada de Pala Trail. The trail goes along the meadow, on the right side, and then a stream. A climb to an old shack follows. Bear right at the shack to get on a barely visible trail, which is the Pala Seca Trail, and then continue for about 2 miles to get back to the Cañada de Pala Trail. Continue the ride by turning right at the intersection with Los Huecos Trail about 5.7 miles after you started the option.

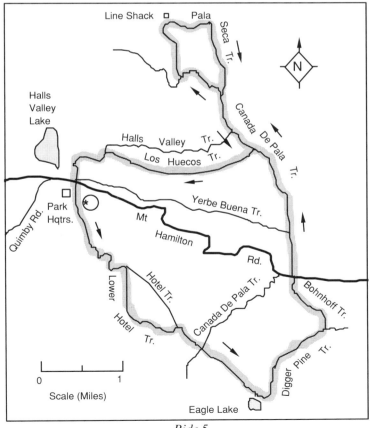

Ride 5

6   **SAN JOSE**
Alum Rock Park

Region: *Santa Clara Valley East*	**Ride Rating:** *Easy*
Total Distance: *9 miles*	**Riding Time:** *1-2 hours*
Total Elevation Gain: *500 Feet*	**Calories Burned:** *300*
Type of Bike: *Mountain Bike*	

Terrain

The trail through Alum Rock Park is sometimes paved and other times is a dirt trail. It is possible to do this ride on a road bike, but the dirt trails sometimes can be a bit rutted, suggesting the use of a mountain bike. The grade is almost flat and there is plenty of shade, resulting in this ride being one of the easiest mountain rides in the area.

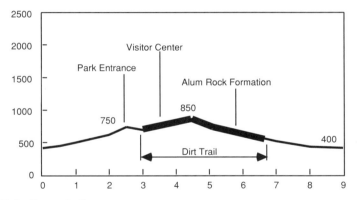

Ride Description

Alum Rock Park is located in the foothills just east of San Jose. It consists of about 700 acres of land used for hiking, horseback riding, cycling, and picnicking. The canyon, sometimes known as "Little Yosemite," is the source of the Penitencia Creek, which runs through it.

The park gets its name from the huge rock which is visible near the entrance to the park and was originally believed to be rich with alum. Later analysis showed this to be incorrect, but the name stuck.

The park experienced its peak popularity in the years from 1890 to 1932, when it was visited extensively for its 27 natural mineral springs. For the modest price of 25 cents, a visitor could ride from downtown San Jose on the Alum Rock Steam Railroad. At the park were a tea garden, indoor swimming pool, dance pavilion, restaurant, and of course, the mineral baths. It was common for visitors to come and spend an entire day at the park and to return on the train at the end of the day.

As the Santa Clara Valley grew and its population expanded, it was no longer practical to keep the park as it was and, in the early 1960's, it was converted to its present form as a natural recreation area, with the natural setting disturbed as little as possible by visitors to the park.

The ride starts at the intersection of Alum Rock Avenue and White Road, about 2.5 miles west of the park entrance. You will get to the park by riding up a slight hill on Alum Rock Avenue. Your tour through the park will take you to the easternmost end of the bike trail in the park and will then bring you back and out on Penitencia Creek Road, at the other park entrance. Penitencia Creek Road will lead you to White Road for the return to your starting point.

Starting Point

Start the ride at the intersection of Alum Rock Avenue and White Road. To get there, take Highway 680 north from San Jose and get off at the Alum Rock Avenue exit. Proceed on Alum Rock Avenue to the intersection with White Road where there are several shopping centers in which to park your car or to meet up with others.

Ride Details and Mile Markers

0.0 Start by heading east on Alum Rock Avenue, toward the park.

1.6 Pass Mt. Hamilton Road intersection, on the right.

1.7 Golf course is on the left.

2.4 Park Entrance at Crothers Road intersection.

2.8 Go under the bridge and look for the trail immediately on the right — a uphill dirt trail. Follow the dirt trail along the creek.

3.5 Visitor Center is on the right. Trail maps are available.

4.0 Cross the bridge — stay on the trail.

4.3 End of trail — turn around and return the way you came.

5.1 Visitor Center is on the left.

5.8 Stay on the trail at the place where you first got on the trail — go over the bridge — Alum Rock formation is on the right.

5.9 Foot trail begins. Go across the road and ride along the road until you see the trail across the bridge at Eagle Rock Picnic Area.

6.6 Clearing — look for the trail continuation on the far right of the clearing.

6.7 Turn left onto Penitencia Creek Road and leave the park.

7.9 Turn left onto White Road.

9.2 Back at the intersection with Alum Rock Avenue.

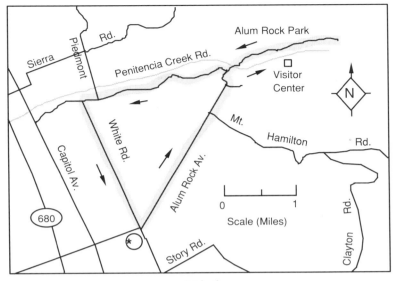

Ride 6

Trail through Alum Rock Park

Photo: Conrad J. Boisvert

Santa Clara Valley: West Foothills

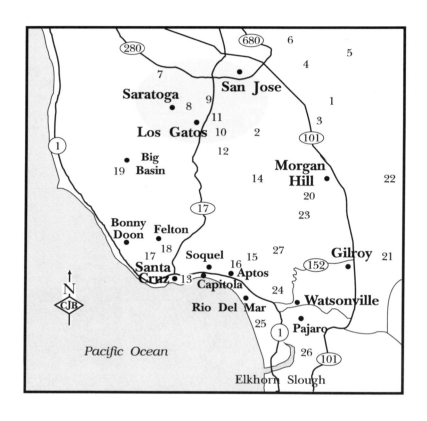

7 SARATOGA
Saratoga and Stevens Canyon Back Roads

Region: Santa Clara Valley West
Total Distance: 14.5 miles
Total Elevation Gain: 700 feet
Type of Bike: Road Bike

Ride Rating: Moderate
Riding Time: 2 hours
Calories Burned: 500

Terrain

There are two hills to climb on this ride, but they are fairly modest and the scenery makes them very worthwhile. Good any time of year, this ride is best in the spring when the streams are at their fullest.

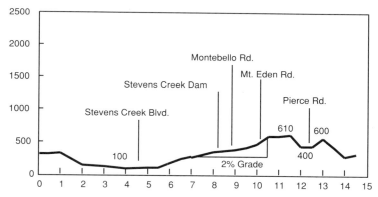

Ride Description

The town of Saratoga serves as the starting point for this ride, which takes you past Stevens Creek Dam and through heavily wooded backroads before returning to Saratoga. In Saratoga, there are a variety of restaurants, bakeries and shops to enjoy after your ride.

Saratoga was originally established by Martin McCarthy in the mid- nineteenth century. Known as McCarthysville until 1863, its name was changed to Saratoga because the presence of the natural springs were reminiscent of those in famous Saratoga Springs, New York.

The first part of the ride is along busy Saratoga-Sunnyvale Road and Stevens Creek Blvd. It then follows Foothill Blvd and Stevens Canyon Road up past the Stevens Creek Dam and Reservoir. Mt. Eden Road, Pierce Road, and Congress Springs Road provide the return route into Saratoga.

Starting Point

Start the ride in Saratoga, near the junction of the four roads, Saratoga Avenue, Saratoga-Sunnyvale Road (Highway 85), Big Basin Way (Highway 9), and Saratoga-Los Gatos Road (also Highway 9). From Highway 280, northwest of San Jose, take the Saratoga-Sunnyvale Road exit and head south on Saratoga-Sunnyvale Road until you reach Saratoga. From Highway 17, south of San Jose, take the exit for Highway 9 (in Los Gatos) and head northwest to Saratoga. Park anywhere near town that is convenient.

Ride Details and Mile Markers

0.0   Proceed out of Saratoga by heading north on Saratoga-Sunnyvale Road. There is a bike lane on this road.

0.6   Saratoga High School is on the right.

1.7   Pierce Road intersection is on the left.

3.8   Road changes name to De Anza Blvd.

4.5   Turn left onto Stevens Creek Blvd.

6.4   Turn left onto South Foothill Blvd.

6.9   Road changes name to Stevens Canyon Road.

8.3   Stevens Creek Dam and Reservoir are on the left.

8.8   Montebello Road intersection is on the right.

10.2   Turn left onto Mt. Eden Road and begin climb.

11.0   Summit of Mt. Eden Road.

12.4   Turn right onto Pierce Road and climb again.

13.0   Summit of Pierce Road.

13.3   Turn left onto Congress Springs Road for downhill into Saratoga.

14.0   Begin Big Basin Way.

14.5   Back in Saratoga.

Extra Option on Montebello Road (5 miles)

At the 8.8 mile mark is the intersection with Montebello Road. At this point, if you wish to add some miles and some elevation gain, you can proceed up Montebello Road. It goes about 5 miles and gains about 2000 feet to its end, so it is not for the timid.

Extra Option to the End of Stevens Canyon Road (4 miles)

At the 10.2 mile mark turn onto Mt. Eden Road. If you stay on Stevens Canyon Road, however, you can go another 4 miles before the road ends. In contrast to the Montebello option, Stevens Canyon Road has the relatively modest elevation gain of about 500 feet to contend with. The grade is not steep and the surroundings are lush forests along Stevens Creek.

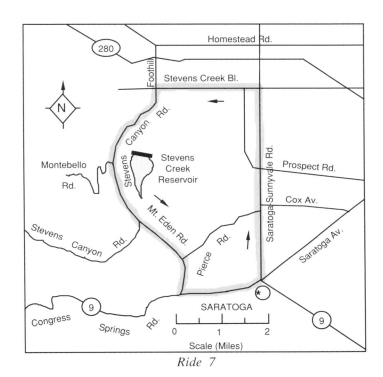

Ride 7

Stevens Canyon Reservoir

Photo: Conrad J. Boisvert

8 LOS GATOS
Los Gatos, Villa Montalvo, and Saratoga

Region: *Santa Clara Valley West*
Total Distance: *13 miles*
Total Elevation Gain: *350 feet*
Type of Bike: *Road Bike*

Ride Rating: *Easy*
Riding Time: *2 hours*
Calories Burned: *300*

Terrain

The majority of the ride is on busy Saratoga-Los Gatos Road (Highway 9). However, there is a bike path along the road for part of the way and although it is on the north side of the road, you can use it going in both directions. Some uphill sections will be encountered, but they are small climbs.

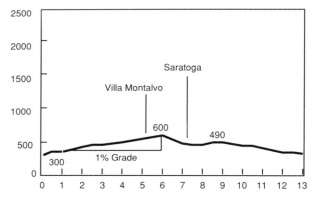

Ride Description

Villa Montalvo, in Saratoga, was the home of U.S. Senator James D. Phelan. At his home, he entertained many opera personalities, legislators, literary people, and dignitaries, starting around 1914. After his death, he left the estate to the San Francisco Art Association, with the intention that it be used for the advancement of the arts, especially relating to the development of promising young students. Today, there is an art gallery, concert amphitheater, gardens, and hiking trails in the hills above the estate, all open to the public.

This ride begins in downtown Los Gatos and leads to Villa Montalvo, and then on into Saratoga. It returns to Los Gatos by reversing the route, without the stop at Villa Montalvo.

Starting Point

The ride starts in Los Gatos. It is usually easy to park near Los Gatos High School. To get there, take the Saratoga Avenue (Highway 9) exit for Los Gatos off State Highway 17. Head east on Saratoga Avenue to the intersection of Los Gatos Blvd. Turn right and proceed on Los Gatos Blvd. (becomes East Main Street) for about 0.5 mile, where the high school will be on the right. Park in the back of the high school or anywhere nearby to begin the ride.

Ride Details and Mile Markers

0.0   Start by heading west on East Main Street, as you leave the high school area.

0.2   Cross the Highway 17 overpass.

0.4   Cross North Santa Cruz Avenue.

0.6   Los Gatos Museum is on the right. Turn right onto Bayview.

0.8   Turn left onto Bean Avenue, then immediately turn right onto Massol Avenue.

1.0   Cross Bachman Avenue.

1.1   Turn left onto Saratoga-Los Gatos Road. This is a very busy road, so you may have to walk your bike across.

2.1   Quito Road intersection.

3.2   Fruitvale Avenue intersection.

4.2   Turn left onto Montalvo Road. There is a short climb up to Villa Montalvo.

4.7   Villa Montalvo entrance portals.

5.1   Villa Montalvo. Park your bike and explore the grounds. When you leave, you will use the continuation of the road on which you came.

5.7   Villa Montalvo exit portals. You are now on Piedmont Road.

6.0   Turn right onto Mendelsohn Lane.

6.2   Turn left to get back onto Saratoga-Los Gatos Road, heading toward Saratoga.

7.1   Turn left onto Big Basin Way. This is the town of Saratoga where there are many fine shops and restaurants for your enjoyment. When you are ready to return to Los Gatos, retrace your route, except for the Villa Montalvo side trip.

13.0   Back at Los Gatos High School.

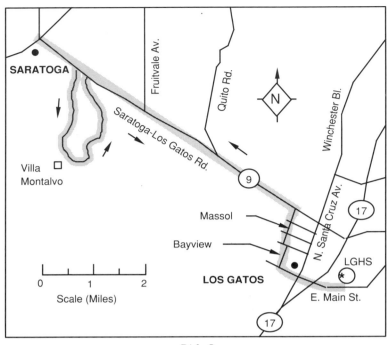

Ride 8

Villa Montalvo in Saratoga

Photo: Conrad J. Boisvert

9 LOS GATOS
Los Gatos Creek Trail

Region: *Santa Clara Valley West*
Total Distance: *13 miles*
Total Elevation Gain: *20 feet*
Type of Bike: *Road Bike*

Ride Rating: *Easy*
Riding Time: *1-2 hours*
Calories Burned: *300*

Terrain

The trail is flat and paved, except for a few sections of dirt or gravel. It is heavily used by walkers, runners, and cyclists, so it is important to be careful and to avoid excessive speeds. Although there is little shade along the way, this ride is very enjoyable any time of the year.

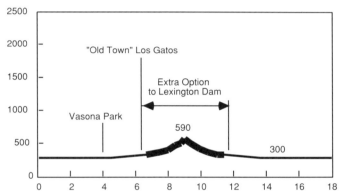

Ride Description

The town of Los Gatos (Spanish for "The Cats") was named as such because the hills above the town were once populated by mountain lions. Today, Los Gatos is the home to many upscale restaurants and shops, and its residential neighborhoods are among the most fashionable in the South Bay. Vasona Park, also located in Los Gatos, is the site of a lake for boating and fishing as well as a small-scale children's railroad, the Billy Jones Wildcat Railroad.

The Los Gatos Creek Trail runs along the Los Gatos Creek from the Pruneyard Shopping Center in Campbell, through Vasona Park, to Los Gatos and continues past Los Gatos to the Lexington Reservoir. The total round-trip length of the trail, from the Pruneyard to Lexington, is about 16 miles, although this ride only covers the trail to Los Gatos and back, a distance of 13 miles. The ride starts at the Pruneyard, where ample parking can be found, and terminates in Los Gatos. The return to the Pruneyard follows the same route back.

Along the way to Los Gatos, you will pass several picnic and play areas and go completely through Vasona Park. Most of the ride is on the trail, which is paved, but occasionally, you will need to use the main roads. Los Gatos has many fine places to eat, as well as art and antique stores ideal for browsing. A good place for a weekend brunch.

Starting Point

The ride starts at the Pruneyard Shopping Center in Campbell. To get there, take the Hamilton Avenue exit off Highway 17 and go in an easterly direction. Turn right on Bascom Avenue and proceed about 0.5 mile to the Pruneyard Shopping Center, on the right. Park in the back on the right, near the access point for the trail.

Ride Details and Mile Markers

0.0 The entry to the bike path is at the north end of the parking lot at the rear of the Pruneyard Center. Get on the path and head south, toward Los Gatos.

0.3 Go under the bridge at Campbell Avenue.

1.4 Cross over the bridge to get on the west side of the creek.

1.7 Restrooms are on the right.

1.8 Pond and park are on the right.

2.3 Observation tower is on the left.

3.3 Get off the trail at Lark Avenue, cross the bridge to resume on the trail on the other side.

3.8 Enter Vasona Park. The dam is on the right.

4.7 Railroad tracks for Billy Jones Wildcat Railroad are off to the left.

4.9 At the trestle, do not cross the bridge, instead cross the tracks and continue on the dirt section of the trail. If you wish to visit the railroad station, go across the trestle, return when you are done and continue on the trail.

5.1 Go under the bridge for Blossom Hill Road.

5.3 Trail ends. Turn right on Roberts Road. Cross the bridge immediately as the road turns to the right.

5.5 Turn left onto University Avenue.

6.3 "Old Town" Los Gatos is on the left, which is marked by a large sign crossing the walkway. When you are ready, return to the Pruneyard by retracing your route.

12.6 Back at the Pruneyard Center.

Extra Option to the Lexington Reservoir and Dam (5 miles)

This extra option will add about 5 miles to your total mileage, with an uphill climb of about 250 feet.

Continue on University Avenue past Old Town Los Gatos to the intersection with East Main Street. Turn left onto East Main and cross over Highway 17. Just over the bridge, on the right side, is the entrance to the continuation of the Los Gatos Creek Trail. Follow this dirt trail for about 1.8 miles to the Lexington Dam. Near the end of the trail, at the foot of the dam, bear left to cross a bridge over the creek, and then bear right to get on the trail up a very steep section leading to the top of the dam. Walk your bike, if necessary, since this section is very difficult to ride. Reverse your route to return to Los Gatos.

Bike path through Vasona Park

Photo: Conrad J. Boisvert

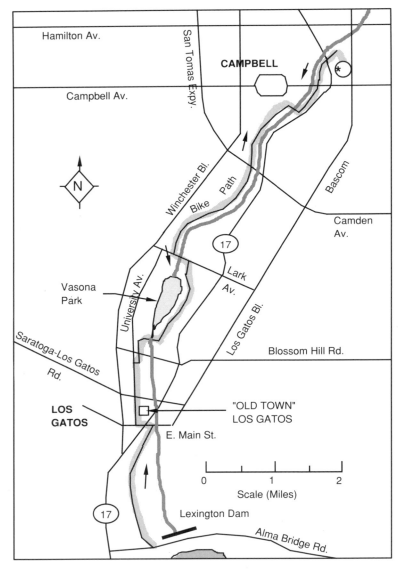

Ride 9

10 LOS GATOS
Sierra Azul Open Space Preserve

	Ride 10A	Ride 10B
Region:	Santa Clara Valley West	
Ride Rating:	Difficult	Moderate
Total Distance:	12 miles	10 miles
Riding Time:	2-3 hours	2 hours
Total Elevation Gain:	2300 feet	1300 feet
Calories Burned:	900	500
Type of Bike:	Mountain	Mountain

Ride Description

The Sierra Azul (Spanish for "Blue Mountains") Open Space Preserve is a large public-use area stretching from Mount Umunhum in the east, to Lexington Reservoir in the west. It was acquired and is managed by the Midpenninsula Open Space District (MPOSD), headquartered in Palo Alto. The trails are along fire roads through the preserve and climb to elevations as high as 2600 feet, offering panoramic views of the Santa Cruz Mountains and the Santa Clara Valley.

The rides are good anytime of year, except when it is cold or windy, or after a recent rain. The mountains are heavily-populated with poison oak, so be careful to avoid contact with any suspicious-looking weeds. Two water bottles and a snack may be required, depending on your own personal needs.

Starting Point

Both rides start at or near Los Gatos High School in Los Gatos. To get there, take the Saratoga Avenue (Highway 9) exit for Los Gatos off State Highway 17. Travel east on Saratoga Avenue to the intersection of Los Gatos Blvd. Turn right and proceed on Los Gatos Blvd (becomes East Main Street) for about 0.5 mile, where the high school will be on the right. Park in the back of the school or nearby.

Ride 10A (Difficult)

Ride 10A takes you on surface roads from the town of Los Gatos to the northern entrance into the preserve, on Kennedy Road, above Los Gatos. From there you cross the entire length of the trail and get out of the preserve at the other end at Lexington Reservoir. You return to Los Gatos on surface roads. This is a very aggressive mountain bike ride. It has 6.5 miles of trail riding in the Sierra Azul Open Space Preserve and another 1.8 miles on the Los Gatos Creek Trail and is intended for advanced mountain bike riders only. The ride begins and ends in Los Gatos, a charming town with lots of good bars, restaurants and coffee houses. It is a popular bicycling center and you are likely to find many other cyclists in town on weekends.

Terrain

Most of the Sierra Azul trail is on a wide fire road with very little shade, except for the last half mile, which is on a narrow single track. There is a total elevation gain of about 2300 feet, including some very steep sections (15-20% for short distances). The roads to and from the preserve can carry substantial car traffic, but bike lanes and wide shoulders make them quite safe.

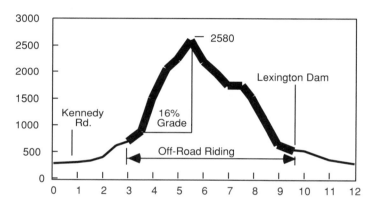

Ride 10A: Ride Details and Mile Markers

0.0   Go east on East Main Street, heading away from the center of Los Gatos. East Main Street becomes Los Gatos Blvd.

0.5   Go straight through the intersection with Saratoga Avenue, coming in from the left.

0.7   Turn right onto Kennedy Road.

3.0   Summit of Kennedy Road — 650 feet. Sierra Azul Open Space Preserve entrance is on the right. Carry your bike over the barrier to get on the trail.

3.6   Steep climb begins.

4.2   Climb becomes less steep.

4.5   Flat spot with shade — then steep up again.

5.4   False summit — very steep just ahead — walk your bike.

5.6   Summit — 2580 feet.

5.7   Bear right at unmarked major split in the trail.

5.8   Begin very steep downhill section.

6.3 Marker on the right indicating preserve boundary.

6.4 Quarry comes into view ahead and off to the right.

6.6 Trail junction off to the left — continue straight ahead.

7.0 Unmarked trail junction, where four trails come together. Turn right to go down single-track trail. This section is very narrow in spots and dense with vegetation.

7.3 Barrier — carry bike across.

8.3 Limekiln Road is visible off to the right. Do not try to get to it, since it is not the road you want.

8.8 Exit Sierra Azul Open Space Preserve at Alma Bridge Road. Turn right on road.

9.6 Top of Lexington Dam. Get on Los Gatos Creek Trail via entry point at the far side of the building on the right.

9.8 Cross over a small bridge.

11.3 Turn right when the trail ends at East Main Street.

11.7 Back at Los Gatos High School.

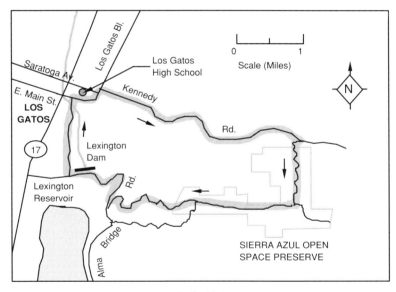

Ride 10A

Ride 10B (Moderate)

Ride 10B also begins and ends in Los Gatos, but does not cover the entire length of the preserve. Instead, you enter the preserve at a trailhead near Lexington Reservoir and exit at another trailhead, also near Lexington. This option covers only a section on the western side of the preserve and requires substantially less climbing.

Terrain

The section of trail covered in this option is in the western portion of the Sierra Azul Open Space Preserve, above Lexington Reservoir. The trail encompasses only a small portion of the preserve, but has a significant hill climb of about 1000 feet on a wide fire trail to challenge you. The downhill return is on a narrow single-track.

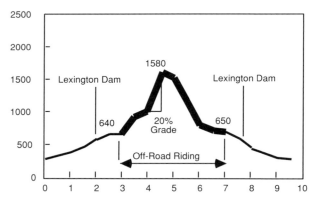

Ride 10B: Ride Details and Mile Markers

0.0 Start by heading west on East Main Street, toward the town of Los Gatos.

0.2 Cross over East Main Street just before the bridge over Highway 17 to get on the Los Gatos Creek Trail. Head south on the trail toward Lexington Reservoir.

1.5 Steep section for a short distance — you may need to walk.

1.8 Bear left across a small bridge and then bear right to go up the steep climb to get to the top of Lexington Dam — walk again.

2.0 Top of the dam. Go left on Alma Bridge Road.

2.6 Limekiln Road (private) intersection is on the left.

2.8 Trailhead for Sierra Azul Open Space Preserve. Do not enter here — this is where you will come out.

3.1 Second trailhead for Sierra Azul Open Space Preserve. Gate is marked with the code, "SA21." Carry your bike over the gate and climb the steep trail.

3.6 Begin flat section of the trail.

3.9 Climb again.

4.1 Steep section.

4.2 Barrier into preserve. Carry your bike over it.

4.4 Summit — 1580 feet.

5.0 Turn left at intersection where four trails merge.

5.3 Barrier — carry your bike over.

6.3 Limekiln Road is just over the creekbed on the right. Stay on the trail and begin uphill climb for a short distance.

6.8 Gate at end of trail — turn right on the Alma Bridge Road.

7.6 Back at Lexington Dam — cross over and turn right onto Los Gatos Creek Trail at the gate on the far side of the building on the right. Steep downhill section — be careful.

7.7 Cross small bridge.

9.4 End of trail at East Main Street — turn right and return to high school.

9.6 Back at Los Gatos High School.

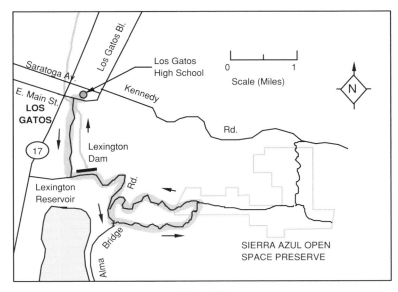

Ride 10B

11 LOS GATOS
St. Joseph's Hill Open Space Preserve

Region: *Santa Clara Valley West*   **Ride Rating:** *Moderate*
Total Distance: *6 miles*   **Riding Time:** *2 hours*
Total Elevation Gain: *700 feet*   **Calories Burned:** *300*
Type of Bike: *Mountain Bike*

Terrain

The trail is very steep in places, but is rated only as a moderate level ride because it is not very long and only climbs 700 feet. Intermediate riders may find it more difficult than they anticipate because of the steepness of the trail.

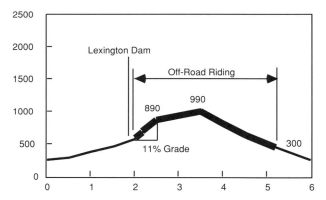

Ride Description

The St. Joseph's Hill Open Space Preserve was acquired from the California Society of the Province of Jesus in 1984 and has recently been opened for public use. Approximately 170 acres are open to the public with the remaining 97 acres serving as an easement between the Open Space Preserve and the Novitiate Winery. At the top of the hill are the remains of the vineyards used by the winery when they grew their own grapes.

The ride starts in Los Gatos and takes the Los Gatos Creek Trail to Lexington Dam and Reservoir, where there is access to the St. Joseph's Hill Open Space Preserve. The ride is good any time of year, except when it is cold. Poison oak is plentiful along the trails, so be cautious and don't touch any of the weeds.

Starting Point

The ride starts at or near Los Gatos High School in Los Gatos. To get there, take the Saratoga Avenue (Highway 9) exit for Los Gatos off State Highway 17. Go east on Saratoga Avenue to the intersection of Los Gatos Blvd. Turn right and proceed on Los Gatos Blvd (which becomes East Main Street) for about 0.5 miles, where the high school will be on the right. Park in the back of the high school or anywhere nearby.

Ride Details and Mile Markers

0.0 Start by heading west on East Main Street, toward the town of Los Gatos.

0.2 Cross over East Main Street just before the bridge over Highway 17 to get on the Los Gatos Creek Trail. Head south on the trail toward Lexington Reservoir.

1.5 Steep section.

1.8 Bear left to go across a small bridge and then bear right to go up the steep climb to get to the top of the Lexington Dam.

2.0 Top of the dam. Go left on Alma Bridge Road.

2.2 On the left side of the road is a gate, the entry to St. Joseph's Hill Open Space Preserve. It is not marked as such, but there is a designation "SJ03" on the gate post. Go around the gate to get on the trail. The beginning of the trail is very steep and narrow, so you may have to walk up this section.

2.7 Turn right at the junction for Jones Trail. From the ridge along this section, you can see the Sierra Azul Open Space Preserve across the canyon below.

3.3 Turn right off Jones Trail and climb up toward St. Joseph's Hill. This section can be rough.

3.4 Turn right onto the double-track and proceed around the top of the hill. Notice the old vineyard posts on the left from a time when the Novitiate Winery grew their own grapes.

3.6 The trail becomes a single-track as Los Gatos High School and the Novitiate Winery come into view below. Continue around and then down the hill.

3.7 Double-track for a short bit.

4.1 Go straight through at the junction with Jones Trail.

4.2 The trail makes a sharp left bend and then climbs steeply.

4.3 Bear right at the trail junction.

4.5 Turn right onto Jones Trail.

4.9 Barrier — you must walk your bike in this section.

5.2 Barrier — resume riding.

5.4 End of trail. Go through the gate and get on Jones Road.

5.6 Turn left onto College Road.

6.0 Turn right onto East Main Street.

6.2 Back at Los Gatos High School.

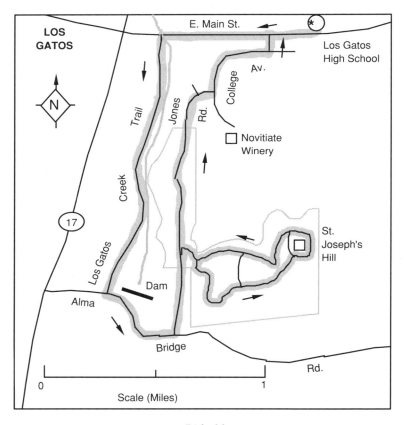

Ride 11

St. Joseph's Hill Open Space Preserve

Santa Cruz Area:
Mountains and Beaches

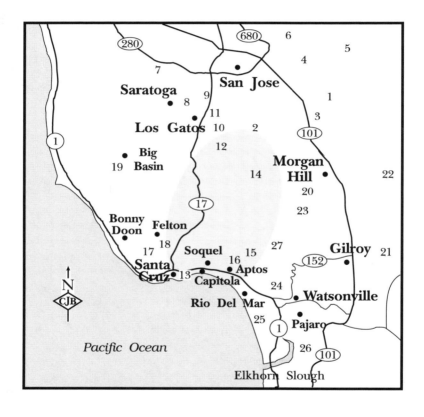

12 SANTA CRUZ
Mountain Charlie Road

Region: *Santa Cruz Area*
Total Distance: *50 miles*
Total Elevation Gain: *2700 feet*
Type of Bike: *Road Bike*

Ride Rating: *Difficult*
Riding Time: *5 hours*
Calories Burned: *1600*

Terrain

This ride has a major hill climb in each direction. The roads are generally not very busy, with the exception of the portion of the ride from Santa Cruz to Soquel, which generally has substantial traffic.

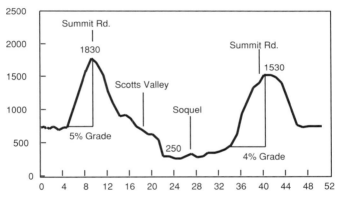

Ride Description

One of the many highlights of this ride is the route it takes along the old Mountain Charlie Road through the Santa Cruz Mountains. Narrow and winding, it is seldom used by cars. Although somewhat bumpy in spots, the pleasures of the cool shade of the deep redwood forests and the splendid mountain scenery make it a cyclist's delight.

"Mountain Charlie" was perhaps the most colorful resident of the Santa Cruz Mountains. An Irishman, Charlie McKiernan came to California in 1850, ostensibly to take part in the gold rush. Instead, he settled in the Santa Cruz Mountains and became the archetypical "mountain man." His cabin was located about a mile from what is now the intersection of Summit Road and Mountain Charlie Road.

Working at various times as a rancher, teamster, road-builder, and stage operator, he is best-known for his encounter with a large grizzly bear, quite common at that time in the mountains. The grizzly crushed

McKiernan's skull in his jaws and left him for dead. He amazingly survived and was fitted with a silver plate to fill the gaping hole in his skull. Although severely disfigured, he lived for many years and was partly responsible for the building of the stage road which today bears his name.

Your route follows Alma Bridge Road around the eastern side of Lexington Reservoir and then climbs on Aldercroft Heights Road, Old Santa Cruz Highway, and finally, Mountain Charlie Road for the steep climb to Summit Road. Along Mountain Charlie Road you can see the steep sections of the road separated by relatively flat portions. The flat sections were intended to rest the stagecoach horses on the long and arduous climb over the mountains.

Summit Road crosses over Highway 17 to reach the continuation of Mountain Charlie Road. Glenwood Drive, Scotts Valley Drive, and Glen Canyon Road lead to Santa Cruz. Soquel Drive then takes you to Soquel for the return climb to Summit Road via Soquel-San Jose Road, and then back to Lexington on Old Santa Cruz Highway, Aldercroft Heights, and Alma Bridge Road.

Starting Point

The ride starts at Lexington Dam, just above Los Gatos. To get there, take Highway 17 south toward Santa Cruz. Exit by turning left at Alma Bridge Road, at the top of Lexington Dam. There is ample parking available at the dam.

Ride Details and Mile Markers

0.0 Proceed east on Alma Bridge Road, away from Highway 17.

0.7 Limekiln Canyon Road is on the left (private road).

2.6 Soda Springs Canyon is on the right.

2.9 Soda Springs Road is on the left.

4.4 Turn right onto Aldercroft Heights Road and begin to climb.

4.9 Turn left onto Old Santa Cruz Highway.

5.1 Go straight at the intersection with Idylwild Road on the right.

6.4 Holy City Road is on the right.

7.6 Turn right onto Mountain Charlie Road — a steep and narrow climb.

8.4 Turn right onto Summit Road and immediately make another right turn to cross over Highway 17.

8.6 Continue straight ahead on Mountain Charlie Road (Summit Road goes to the right). Historical marker is on the right.

9.5 Mountain Charlie's cabin is on the left with an historical marker.

13.9 Turn right onto Glenwood Drive.

14.9 Bean Creek Road is on the right.

16.8 Turn right onto Scotts Valley Drive.

18.7 Turn left onto Mount Hermon Road, and then take the first left turn onto Glen Canyon Road.

19.3 Cross under Highway 17.

19.4 Bear right at the intersection to stay on Glen Canyon Road.

22.4 Turn right onto Branciforte Drive.

23.6 Continue straight through at Goss Avenue — Branciforte becomes Market Street.

23.9 Turn left onto Water Street.

24.5 Turn right at Poplar Avenue and then left onto Soquel Avenue.

25.9 Cross over Highway 1 and begin Soquel Drive.

27.6 Turn left at Soquel-San Jose Road (Old San Jose Road).

30.9 Casalegno's Country Store is on the left.

33.1 Begin to climb more steeply.

37.7 Miller Hill Road is on the right.

39.0 Turn left onto Summit Road.

39.3 Summit Center is on the right.

41.8 Turn right onto Old Santa Cruz Highway.

42.9 Mountain Charlie Road intersection is on the left.

45.4 Continue straight through at Idylwild Road.

45.6 Turn right onto Aldercroft Heights Road.

46.1 Turn left onto Alma Bridge Road.

50.5 Ride ends at Lexington Dam.

Mountain Charlie Road   Photo: Conrad J. Boisvert

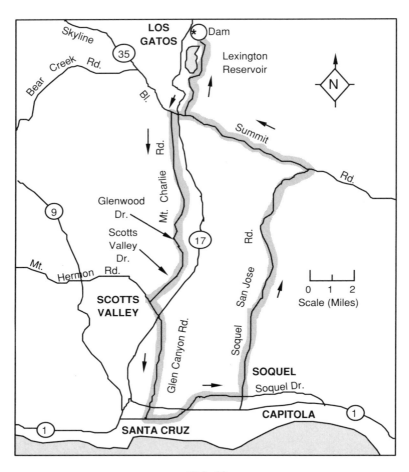

Ride 12

13 SANTA CRUZ
Santa Cruz and Capitola Beach Ride

Region: *Santa Cruz Area*
Total Distance: *23 miles*
Total Elevation Gain: *400 feet*
Type of Bike: *Road Bike*

Ride Rating: *Easy*
Riding Time: *2-3 hours*
Calories Burned: *600*

Terrain

The roads are quite flat, except for several small hills. There can be substantial traffic, especially on summer weekends, but bike lanes provided over most of the roads make the ride quite safe.

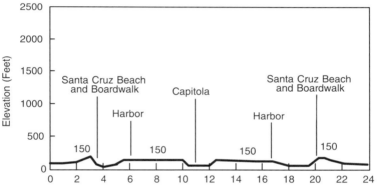

Ride Description

Both Santa Cruz and Capitola have long been popular beach resorts for Northern California. This ride follows a leisurely and picturesque route along the coast from Natural Bridges State Park, just north of Santa Cruz, to Capitola, and then returns along the same route.

There are many diversions along the way, so it is suggested that you plan to spend the better part of the day fully exploring them. This ride is good any time of year, but is especially nice on weekdays and during the off-season, when traffic is minimal. Be advised to bring a jacket or windbreaker, as the coast can be quite cool, even when inland temperatures are high.

Starting Point

Plenty of free parking is available along the streets near the rear entrance to Natural Bridges State Park on Delaware Avenue, at the intersection with Natural Bridges Road. To get there, proceed north from Santa Cruz on Highway 1. Just before leaving town, turn left onto Swift Street. Go about ½-mile and then turn right onto Delaware Avenue. Continue another ½-mile to Natural Bridges Road intersection.

Ride Details and Mile Markers

0.0   On Delaware Avenue, head south toward Santa Cruz. [**Option:** Go through Natural Bridges State Park by way of the rear gate on Delaware Avenue. This brings you out at West Cliff Drive.]

0.2   Turn right onto Swanton Blvd., heading toward the ocean.

0.6   Turn left onto West Cliff Drive — follow the bike path.

2.4   Lighthouse and Seal Rock are on the right.

3.3   Santa Cruz Wharf is on the right. Continue straight ahead onto Beach Street. [**Option:** Ride on wharf out and back.]

3.5   Santa Cruz beach and boardwalk.

3.7   Turn left onto Riverside Drive.

3.8   Bear to the left to Liebrandt.

4.0   Continue straight across Third Street. This is a one-way street against your direction, but there is a bike path on the right, just across the intersection. The street name becomes Laurel Street Extension.

4.2   Turn right onto Front Street.

4.3   Turn right onto Laurel Street and cross over the bridge. Note that Laurel Street becomes Broadway at this point.

4.4   Turn right onto River Levee Bikeway, just over the bridge.

4.9   End of bikeway. Turn right onto East Cliff Drive and climb the hill.

5.1   Turn right to stay on East Cliff Drive.

5.4   Museum is on the left side.

5.5   Turn right onto Seabright Avenue, then turn left to go along the path on the edge of the cliff.

5.7   Turn left onto Fourth Avenue, then left again onto Atlantic Avenue.

5.9   Turn right onto Seabright Avenue.

6.0   Turn right onto Murray Street.

6.2   Cross the bridge — the harbor is on the right.

6.3   Turn right onto Lake Avenue.

6.7   Turn left onto East Cliff Drive.

6.8   Turn right to stay on East Cliff Drive.

7.7   Turn right again to stay on East Cliff Drive.

9.4   Turn right onto Opal Cliff Drive.

10.1   Turn right onto Portola Drive (becomes Stockton Avenue).

10.5   Enter the town of Capitola.

11.8   Leave Capitola on Stockton Avenue. Return to Santa Cruz by backtracking your route.

22.0   End of ride, back at Natural Bridges.

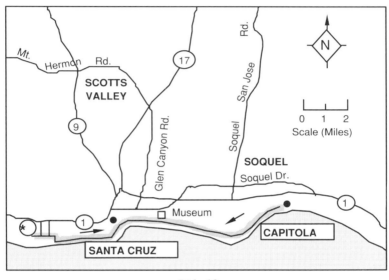

Ride 13

Santa Cruz Yacht Harbor   Photo: Conrad J. Boisvert

14 SANTA CRUZ
Along the Crest of Summit Road

	Ride 14A	Ride 14B
Region:	Santa Cruz Area	
Ride Rating:	Easy	Difficult
Total Distance:	7 miles	37 miles
Riding Time:	1 hour	3-4 hours
Total Elevation Gain:	800 feet	3300 feet
Calories Burned:	300	1500
Type of Bike:	Road Bike	Road Bike

Terrain

Ride 14A has a single hill climb on a lightly traveled road and a short section of dirt road. Ride 14B is a much longer ride and has substantial climbing with a long section of Summit Road being rough and unpaved.

Ride Description

Before the Loma Prieta Earthquake of October 17, 1989, the Summit Center store on Summit Road was a focal point for bicyclists traveling the Santa Cruz Mountain roads. It served as the starting point or as a rest stop along the rugged and steep roads throughout the area. The earthquake severely damaged the structure of the store and left it closed indefinitely. However, you can still use the store's parking lot as the start and finish of rides along the mountain crest.

Both rides travel along the mountaintop. Loma Prieta Mountain is the highest mountain in the Santa Cruz Range, with an altitude of 3806 feet. Ride 14A is an easy loop, with only a small amount of climbing, excellent for the novice rider or for someone not desiring a big workout.

Ride 14B, on the other hand, provides a substantial challenge, with lots of climbing and 24 miles on dirt trails. It covers the same roads as Ride 14A, with the extra option of a 15-mile jaunt to Mt. Madonna State Park, at the other end of Summit Road.

Starting Point

The Summit Center Store is on Summit Road, east of Highway 17. To get there, take Highway 17 south toward Santa Cruz and get off at the Summit Road exit. Follow Summit Road east for about 3.5 miles, where you will find the store on the left side, just past the Loma Prieta Avenue intersection.

Ride 14A (Easy)

The Summit Center Store is on Summit Road, just a few miles east of Highway 17. From the store, go west only about 0.2 mile and get on Loma Prieta Avenue. Here, you will climb with an elevation gain of about 800 feet over a distance of about 3 miles, a rather modest average grade of around 5%. The road will take you through orchards and by Christmas tree farms and will offer some spectacular views, one of the true joys of cycling. The last part of Loma Prieta Avenue is a dirt road, but road bike tires are no problem, as it is quite smooth. You will return by dropping steeply down Mt. Bache Road to connect with Highland Way, which becomes Summit Road, for your downhill return to the store.

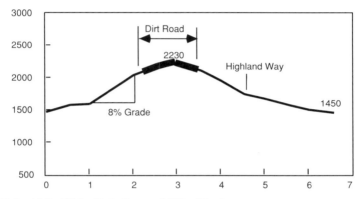

Ride 14A: Ride Details and Mile Markers

0.0   From Summit Center Store, proceed west on Summit Road.

0.2   Turn right onto Loma Prieta Avenue. Climb uphill past orchards and Christmas tree farms.

2.2   Dirt section of road begins.

3.5   Turn right onto Mt. Bache Road (may not be marked). This is a paved road and goes steeply downhill.

4.5   Bear right at the intersection with Highland Way.

5.7   Skyland Road intersection is on the left.

6.1   Soquel-San Jose Road intersection is on the left.

6.5   Back at Summit Center Store.

Ride 14B (Difficult)

This ride also starts at the store and travels up Loma Prieta Avenue. However, the route takes you left at Mt. Bache Road and continues steeply uphill, continuing onto Loma Prieta Road and then to Summit Road. This part of Summit Road is an unpaved dirt road and is barricaded by a gate across the road. You can easily carry your bike over the gate. This is a public road, but the lands along it are private and sometimes the residents there may not take too kindly to other people touring by. If you consider this and respect the privacy of the residents, you will not have any difficulties. The ride along Summit Road offers panoramic views both east and west and, on a clear day, you seemingly can see forever.

Past the gate at the other end, the road is again paved and leads downhill to intersect with Pole Line Road. About a mile up the hill on Pole Line Road is Mt. Madonna State Park, a good place to rest and enjoy a snack, you may have brought with you before you head back the way you came. After returning over the dirt section of Summit Road, you will continue on Loma Prieta Road and Mt. Bache Road and return to the store via Highland Way and then Summit Road.

This ride is good any time of year except after a rain, when the dirt roads may be a bit messy. You should also keep in mind that this altitude can be 20-30 degrees cooler than at sea level, so bring along warm clothing, especially in the winter.

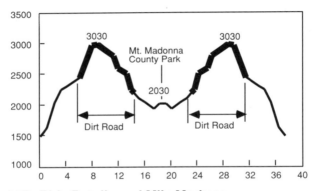

Ride 14B: Ride Details and Mile Markers

0.0   From Summit Center store, proceed west on Summit Road.

0.2   Turn right onto Loma Prieta Avenue. Climb uphill past orchards and Christmas tree farms.

2.2   Dirt section of road begins.

3.5   Turn left onto Loma Prieta Road. This is not well-marked, but is the end of the road. It is paved and climbs immediately.

5.8   Dirt road begins.

6.5   Turn right at Summit Road intersection on right. Carry your bike across the gate.

9.8   Ormsby Cutoff is on the right.

14.0 Gate at other end of Summit Road dirt section.

17.5 Go straight through at intersection with Mt. Madonna Road and Pole Line Road to get on Pole Line Road. Climb the hill.

18.5 Mt. Madonna State Park. Return down Pole Line Road.

23.0 Gate to Summit Road dirt section.

30.5 Gate at other end of Summit Road. Turn left onto Loma Prieta Road.

31.2 Paved road begins.

33.5 Begin Mt. Bache Road at the intersection with Loma Prieta Avenue.

34.5 Bear right onto Highland Way.

35.7 Skyland Road intersection is on the left.

36.1 Soquel-San Jose Road intersection is on the left.

36.5 Back at the Summit Center store.

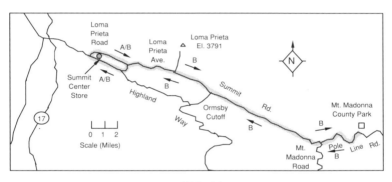

Ride 14

Orchards along Loma Prieta Avenue   Photo: Conrad J. Boisvert

15 SOQUEL
Eureka Canyon and Soquel Loop

Region: *Santa Cruz Area*
Total Distance: *40 miles*
Total Elevation Gain: *2700 feet*
Type of Bike: *Road Bike*

Ride Rating: *Difficult*
Riding Time: *4 hours*
Calories Burned: *1400*

Terrain

Although there is usually substantial traffic between Soquel and Corralitos, the wide shoulder will ensure that you have plenty of room. There is a long and steady hill climb with a relatively modest grade on Eureka Canyon Road, followed by a long downhill on smooth and wide Soquel San Jose Road.

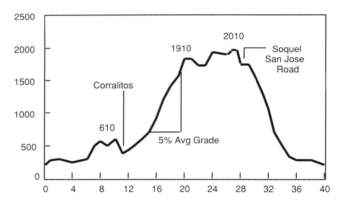

Ride Description

Start this ride in the town of Soquel, just inland from the seaside resort of Capitola. There are several restaurants, antique stores, and a winery (Bargetto Winery), in Soquel for you to enjoy at the conclusion of your ride. This is a difficult ride, with a long uphill climb on Eureka Canyon Road.

The ride starts by heading south and east from Soquel on Soquel Drive. Trout Gulch Road will get you off busy Soquel Drive and take you along rural roads, Valencia Road and Day Valley Road, and connect with Freedom Blvd. for the short hop to Hames Road. Hames Road, another lightly traveled country road, will lead to the little town of Corralitos.

At Corralitos, there is a small country grocery store where you will probably encounter other bicyclists, since it is a major hub for the many beautiful roads around the area favored by local riders. From Corralitos, you will head up Eureka Canyon Road, a steady climb of about 1700 feet on a reasonably gentle grade. This ride starts out through rustic residential areas, dotted with orchards along the Corralitos Creek, and eventually becomes more lush with redwoods, oaks, and madrone as it climbs toward the crest.

Along the crest of Eureka Canyon Road, the road gets a bit rougher as you view the Forest of the Nisene Marks across the valley on the left. Your return to Soquel is down Soquel San Jose Road, a long steady cruise on a smooth, wide road with few turns and little braking required — a just reward for your climbing efforts.

Be sure to bring a windbreaker for the downhill, especially in the winter months, when the temperatures at the top of the mountain can be cooler than down below.

Starting Point

The town of Soquel is the starting point for this ride. To get there, take Highway 1 south from Santa Cruz and get off at the Capitola — Soquel exit. Turn left onto Porter Street, passing under the highway. Continue to Soquel Drive (about 0.4 mile past the highway underpass). Park anywhere around this intersection.

Ride Details and Mile Markers

0.0   Leave Soquel by heading southeast on Soquel Drive.
2.0   Cabrillo College campus.
3.7   Turn left onto Trout Gulch Road.
4.2   Turn right onto Valencia Road.
6.7   Turn left onto Day Valley Road.
8.7   Turn left onto Freedom Blvd.
8.9   Turn left onto Hames Road.
11.0 Turn left onto Eureka Canyon Road at the main intersection in Corralitos. The grocery store is on the right corner. There are rolling hills with slight climb for the next 2 miles.
13.2 Rider Road intersection is on the left.
15.8 Lower Highland Way is on the left.
16.4 Koinonia Conference Grounds is on the left.
20.5 False summit — 1910 feet elevation. Downhill section begins.
22.5 Begin to climb again.
21.8 Camp Loma.
26.5 Spanish Ranch Road is on theleft.

26.8   Summit at Mt. Bache Road intersection. Begin downhill section.
27.9   Skyland Road intersection is on the left.
28.2   Turn left onto Soquel-San Jose Road.
28.5   Begin main downhill run into Soquel.
28.7   Miller Cutoff is on the left.
29.7   Miller Road is on the left.
30.1   Redwood Lodge Road is on the right.
30.6   Stetson Road is on the left.
36.1   Laurel Glen Road is on the right.
39.2   Soquel High School is on the right.
39.5   End of ride in Soquel.

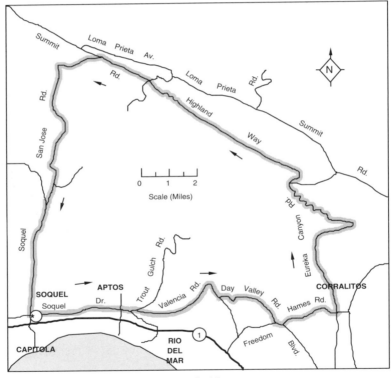

Ride 15

16

APTOS
Forest of Nisene Marks State Park

	Ride 16A	Ride 16B	Ride 16C
Region:	*Santa Cruz Area*		
Ride Rating:	*Easy*	*Moderate*	*Difficult*
Total Distance:	*10 miles*	*22 miles*	*31 miles*
Riding Time:	*1-2 hours*	*3 hours*	*4 hours*
Total Elevation Gain:	*120 feet*	*1500 feet*	*2500 feet*
Calories Burned:	*225*	*800*	*1200*
Type of Bike:	*Mountain*	*Mountain*	*Mountain*

Terrain

Each of these three rides through the park is along unpaved fire roads. There is progressively more climbing required from the easiest to the most difficult of the three. The roads, although quite wide, can carry significant car traffic.

Ride Description

The Forest of Nisene Marks State Park in Aptos is the location of this set of three mountain bike rides. The property was once owned by the Loma Prieta Lumber Company and was logged extensively from 1883-1923. The last remnants of the mill are still visible along the Aptos Creek Fire Road inside the park.

In the 1950s, the Marks family purchased the property. In 1963, the property was donated to the State of California by the Marks children, in memory of their mother, Nisene. The conditions of the deed state that the park is to be operated as a semi-wilderness, and to that end, all trails and fire roads are unpaved and facilities are limited to picnic areas and primitive campgrounds.

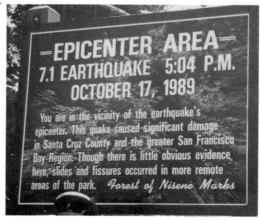

Each of these rides enters the park along the main access road, Aptos Creek Road, which can be reached off Soquel Drive in Aptos. The uphill climbs are all on reasonable grades. There are some steep downhills, but careful riding will permit you to negotiate them. The fact that all rides follow the same starting route allows you to decide the level of ride you want as you go along.

Starting Point

Start at the Coffee Roasting Company in Aptos. To get there go south from Santa Cruz on Highway 1. Get off at the Seacliff Beach-Aptos exit and turn left onto State Park Drive. Turn right onto Soquel Drive and go into the shopping center on the right side (Safeway store). Look for the coffee roasting company store. Arrive a few minutes early and have coffee and a muffin before you begin the ride.

Ride 16A (Easy)

This ride is the easiest of the three and covers about 10 miles with very little climbing. It takes you into the park along Aptos Creek Fire Road to the epicenter marker for the October 1989 Loma Prieta Earthquake. This ride is quite flat and follows Aptos Creek through the redwood forest and past the former mill site.

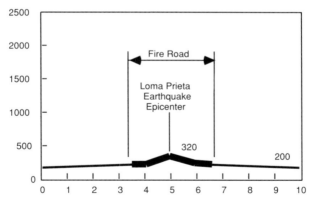

Ride 16A: Ride Details and Mile Markers

0.0 Leave the shopping center by turning right onto Soquel Drive.

0.2 Bear left under the railroad trestle to stay on Soquel Drive.

0.4 Turn left onto Aptos Creek Road and cross over the railroad tracks as you continue down the road and into the park.

2.2 Picnic area is on the right.

2.3 Cross the bridge.

3.3 Porter Family Picnic Area — gate to the Aptos Creek Fire Road is on the left.

3.6 Cross Aptos Creek.

3.9 Loma Prieta Mill Site is on the left.

4.8 Bridge over the creek.

4.9 Loma Prieta Earthquake epicenter marker is on the right. Retrace your route back to your car.

9.8 Back at shopping center.

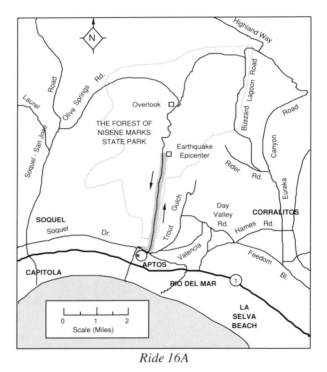

Ride 16A

Ride 16B (Moderate)

This intermediate-level ride covers about 22 miles with 1500-foot elevation gain. It follows the same route as the easy ride, but continues past the epicenter and climbs to the Sand Point Overlook. From there, the route takes you down along the western slope of the park and crosses several streams as it leads to Olive Springs Road and then to Soquel-San Jose Road. The ride into Soquel and then back to Aptos along Soquel Drive has numerous restaurants where you may want to stop.

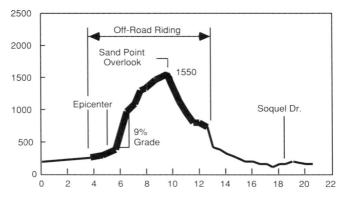

Ride 16B: Ride Details and Mile Markers

0.0   Leave the shopping center by turning right onto Soquel Drive.

0.2   Bear left under the railroad trestle to stay on Soquel Drive.

0.4   Turn left onto Aptos Creek Road and cross over the railroad tracks as you continue down the road and into the park.

2.2   Picnic area is on the right.

2.3   Cross the bridge.

3.3   Porter Family Picnic Area — gate to the Aptos Creek Fire Road is on the left.

3.6   Cross Aptos Creek.

3.9   Loma Prieta Mill Site is on the left.

4.8   Bridge over the creek.

4.9   Loma Prieta Earthquake epicenter marker is on the right.

5.0   Begin steady climb.

6.5   Climb becomes less steep.

9.4   Bear left onto the trail at Sand Point Overlook (toward Olive Springs Road).

9.9   West Ridge Trail Camp is on the right.

10.2   Steep downhill section.

10.9   Gate.

11.0   Bear right at the trail split — trail gets narrower.

11.4   Turn right onto fire road.

12.3   Stream crossings — may be wet.

12.6   Last stream crossing, then climbs steeply for ashort distance.

12.7   Gate. Turn left onto Olive Springs Road.

14.0   Turn left onto Soquel-San Jose Road.

15.1   Casalegno's Country Store is on the right.

18.5   Turn left onto Soquel Drive — busy with traffic.

20.2   Cabrillo College.

21.7   End of ride, back at shopping center.

Ride 16C (Difficult)

This most difficult ride climbs a total of 2500 feet and covers 31 miles. Like the intermediate ride, it also follows the main road past the epicenter and up to the Sand Point Overlook. At this point, however, the route continues climbing to the Santa Rosalia peak, the highest point in the park with an elevation of 2637 feet. The very steep descent along the eastern slope takes you down Buzzard Lagoon Trail and eventually connects with Eureka Canyon Road to bring you into Corralitos. From there, you follow country roads back to Aptos.

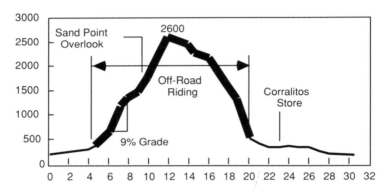

Ride 16C: Ride Details and Mile Markers

0.0   Leave the shopping center by turning right onto Soquel Drive.

0.2   Bear left under the railroad trestle to stay on Soquel Drive.

0.4   Turn left onto Aptos Creek Road and cross over the railroad tracks as you continue down the road and into the park.

2.2   Picnic area is on the right.

2.3   Cross the bridge.

3.3   Porter Family Picnic Area — gate to the Aptos Creek Fire Road is on the left.

3.6   Cross Aptos Creek.

3.9   Loma Prieta Mill Site is on the left.

4.8   Bridge over the creek.

4.9   Loma Prieta Earthquake epicenter marker is on the right.

5.0   Begin steady climb.

6.5   Climb becomes less steep.

9.4 Bear right onto trail at Sand Point Overlook and continue climbing.

11.7 Summit — 2600 feet.

13.6 Gate.

14.7 Turn right at trail intersection onto Buzzard Lagoon Trail.

19.0 Extremely steep downhill section with lots of ruts and loose dirt — be very careful.

19.7 Paved road begins.

20.0 Turn left onto Rider Road, then turn right a short distance later onto Eureka Canyon Road.

23.2 Turn right onto Hames Road at Corralitos — climb the hill.

24.7 Road bends to the right and then to the left — stay on Hames Road.

25.4 Turn right onto Freedom Blvd.

25.5 Turn right onto Day Valley Road — climb the hill.

27.5 Turn right onto Valencia Road.

30.2 Turn left onto Trout Gulch Road.

30.7 Turn right onto Soquel Drive.

31.2 End of ride, back at the shopping center.

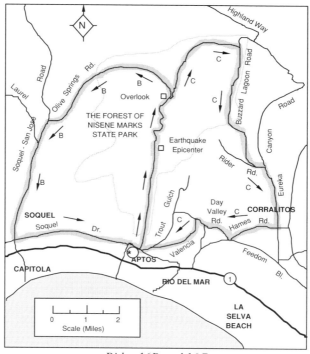

Rides 16B and 16C

West Santa Cruz Area:
Mountains and Forests

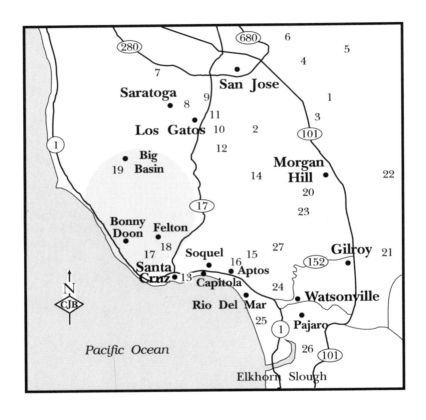

280 680 6 5
4
7
Saratoga   San Jose
          9   1
      8   3
          11
Los Gatos 10   2   101
1
          12
      Big   Morgan
      Basin   Hill   22
19   14   20
                              23
17
Bonny Felton
Doon   27   Gilroy 21
  17 18 Soquel   15   152
          16
Santa   Aptos
Cruz 13 Capitola
              24
Rio Del Mar
              25   Pajaro
N
CJB
Pacific Ocean   26 101

Elkhorn Slough

17 SANTA CRUZ
Empire Grade and Bonny Doon Loop

	Ride 17A	Ride 17B
Region:	West Santa Cruz Area	
Ride Rating:	Moderate	Moderate
Total Distance:	27 miles	32 miles
Riding Time:	3 hours	3.5 hours
Total Elevation Gain:	1800 feet	2100 feet
Calories Burned:	1000	1200
Type of Bike:	Road Bike	Road Bike

Terrain

The hill climbs are on smooth roads with a fairly moderate steepness, but climbs over long distances.

Ride Description

The campus of the University of California, Santa Cruz, is one of the highlights of this pair of rides. It is situated on land which was formerly owned by Henry Cowell, who operated a lime and cement company and a cattle ranch on it. A 2000-acre parcel of the land was sold to the University of California system in 1961. The campus architecture has been purposely designed to blend in with the natural environment of the site. Some of the original buildings on the ranch have been restored and are plainly visible as you tour the campus.

Each of these rides follows roughly the same route. They both start at Natural Bridges State Park in Santa Cruz, follow Empire Grade up a long hill climb, return to the coast on Bonny Doon Road, and return to Santa Cruz along the coast on the Pacific Coast Highway. Each goes past the U.C. Santa Cruz campus on the way up and travels along mountain roads with very little traffic.

Starting Point

Plenty of free parking is available along the streets near the rear entrance to Natural Bridges State Park on Delaware Avenue, at the intersection with Natural Bridges Road. To get there, proceed north out of Santa Cruz on Highway 1. Just before leaving town, turn left onto Swift Street. Go about ½-mile, turn right onto Delaware Avenue, and continue on another ½-mile to the intersection at Natural Bridges Road.

Ride 17A (Moderate)

Ride 17A is the easier of the two and climbs to about 1000 feet on Empire Grade to connect with Smith Grade. Smith Grade goes down and then up for about 500 feet to meet with Bonny Doon Road for a nice downhill back to the coast. The return to Santa Cruz is along the relatively flat Pacific Coast Highway and is usually assisted by a prevailing westerly tailwind.

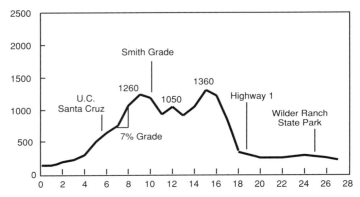

Ride 17A: Ride Details and Mile Markers

0.0 On Delaware Avenue, go south, toward Santa Cruz.

0.2 Turn right onto Swanton Blvd, heading toward the ocean.

0.6 Turn left onto West Cliff Drive — follow the bike path.

2.4 Lighthouse and Seal Rock are on the right.

3.1 Turn left onto Bay Street.

4.1 Cross Mission Street (Highway 1) and climb a bit.

5.1 Turn Left at High Street — High Street becomes Empire Grade.

5.8 U.C. Santa Cruz is on the right.

6.4 Heller Drive is on the right.

7.6 Waldorf School.

10.1 Turn left onto Smith Grade. [Ride 17B continues straight ahead at this point].

10.4 Steep downhill begins.

12.1 Climb for about 1 mile.

13.8 Road turns sharply.

15.3 Turn left onto Bonny Doon Road — downhill all the way to the coast.

16.9 Ocean view ahead and to the right.

18.6 Turn left onto busy Pacific Coast Highway (Highway 1).

25.1 Wilder Ranch Cultural Preserve (State Park) on right side.

26.6   Turn right onto Shaffer Road, then left onto Mission Street, just after entering Santa Cruz city limits.

26.9   Turn right onto Natural Bridges Drive.

27.2   End of ride at Delaware Avenue.

Ride 17B (Moderate)

Ride 17B is the harder of the two rides and climbs all the way up to Pine Flat Road, with about a 1900-foot elevation gain, from where it makes a straight descent in about 7 miles to Bonny Doon Beach on the coast. Return along the Pacific Coast Highway back to Santa Cruz. This downhill ride is surely one of the longest and most enjoyable rides in the South Bay Area.

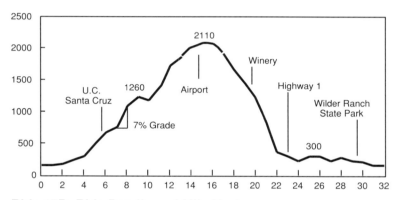

Ride 17B: Ride Details and Mile Markers

0.0   On Delaware Avenue, go south, toward Santa Cruz.

0.2   Turn right onto Swanton Blvd, heading toward the ocean.

0.6   Turn left onto West Cliff Drive — follow the bike path.

2.4   Lighthouse and Seal Rock are on the right side.

3.1   Turn left onto Bay Street.

4.1   Cross Mission Street (Highway 1) and climb a bit.

5.1   Turn Left at High Street — High Street becomes Empire Grade.

5.8   U.C. Santa Cruz is on the right.

6.4   Heller Drive is on the right.

7.6   Waldorf School.

10.1   Smith Grade intersection is on the left.

10.6   Steep uphill grade for about ½-mile.

11.6   Another steep section.

13.5 Intersection with Ice Cream Grade is on the left, Felton Empire Road on right.

14.6 Airport is on the left.

15.5 Turn left onto Pine Flat Road — begin downhill.

17.5 Intersection with Bonny Doon Road is on the right.

17.7 Intersection with Ice Cream Grade is on the left.

19.3 Intersection with Martin Road is on the left.

19.4 Bonny Doon Winery is on the left, Bonny Doon Road is on the right. (Pine Flat Road becomes Bonny Doon Road at this point.)

19.8 Intersection with Smith Grade is on the left.

21.4 Ocean view is ahead and to the right.

23.1 Turn left onto busy Pacific Coast Highway (Highway 1).

29.6 Wilder Ranch Cultural Preserve (State Park) is on the right.

31.1 Turn right onto Shaffer Road, then left onto Mission Street, just after entering Santa Cruz city limits.

31.4 Turn right onto Natural Bridges Drive.

31.7 End of ride at Delaware Avenue.

Highway 1 near Bonny Doon
Photo: Conrad J. Boisvert

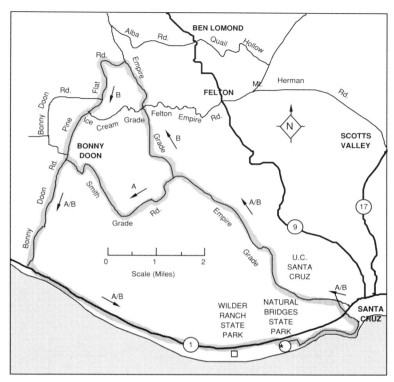

Rides 17A and 17B

18   FELTON
Henry Cowell Redwoods State Park

Region: *North of Santa Cruz*
Total Distance: *8 miles*
Total Elevation Gain: *700 Feet*
Type of Bike: *Mountain Bike*

Ride Rating: *Easy*
Riding Time: *2 hours*
Calories Burned: *350*

Terrain

The ride follows a paved service road, unpaved fire roads, and single-track trails, with a few steep sections.

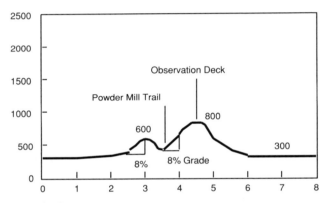

Ride Description

Henry Cowell Redwoods State Park was once part of the Rancho Cañada del Rincon, an 1843 Mexican land grant. A portion of the land was purchased by Henry Cowell and Joseph Warren Welch in the 1860s. Both men had a strong interest in protecting the giant coastal redwoods found there. In 1930, Welch gave part of the property to the County of Santa Cruz and, in 1954, Henry Cowell's son, Samuel, donated another 1500 acres. The land was combined along with other purchases to total approximately 4000 acres, comprising today's park.

This ride starts in the town of Felton, located just outside the park. You will ride on Highway 9 to the park entrance and enter the park, continuing to the main concession area. The ride through the park starts out on a paved service road, Pipeline Road, and leads you deep into the park about 3 miles, to the point at which you will get on a dirt trail, Powder Mill Trail, for some off-road riding.

Powder Mill Trail climbs and then connects to Ridge Trail, which takes you past an observation deck, a great place to relax and enjoy the panoramic views. If you bring along a snack, this is the perfect place to eat it. Ridge Trail continues and connects back with Pipeline Road for the return to the park concession area.

This is a good ride for beginning to intermediate riders who are not quite ready for more challenging rides. There are other trails which you might want to explore on foot as well, particularly Redwood Loop, located near the Nature Center.

Starting Point

To avoid a car-use parking fee at the park, start the ride in the town of Felton, about ½-mile up the road from the park entrance. To get there, take Highway 17 south out of San Jose toward Santa Cruz, and get off at the Mount Herman Road exit. Mount Herman Road ends at Graham Hill Road, where you turn right and immediately join Highway 9 in Felton. There are a number of shopping areas where you can park your car.

Ride Details and Mile Markers

0.0   Go south on Highway 9 away from Felton.

0.6   Turn left into Cowell Redwoods State Park entrance.

1.2   Park Headquarters.

1.4   Restrooms and store. Look for a road going around the back of the restrooms. This is Pipeline Road. Get on this roaad and head south, away from the parking area.

1.5   Nature Center is to the left.

2.0   Cross under the railroad tracks.

2.5   Intersection with Rincon Trail is on the right.

2.9   Continue straight through where Ridge Trail crosses.

3.7   Turn left onto Powder Mill Trail.

4.3   Turn left onto Ridge Trail, head toward observation deck.

4.5   Observation deck is on the right. Trail continues straight ahead.

5.0   Turn right onto Pipeline Road.

5.4   Intersection with Rincon Trail is on the left.

5.9   Railroad tracks.

6.5   Turn left onto road at parking lot.

7.3   Turn right on Highway 9.

7.9   Back in Felton.

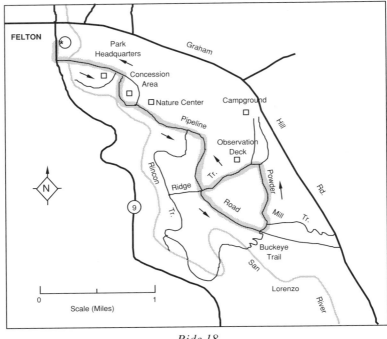

FELTON

Park
Headquarters

Graham

Concession
Area

□ Nature Center

Campground

Hill

Pipeline

Observation
Deck

Rincon

Ridge

Powder

Tr.

9

Tr.

Road

Mill

Tr.

Buckeye
Trail

San

Lorenzo

River

N

0   1
Scale (Miles)

Ride 18

Cowell Redwoods Park

Photo: Conrad J. Boisvert

19 BIG BASIN
Big Basin Redwoods State Park

Region: *West Santa Cruz Area*
Total Distance: *13 miles*
Total Elevation Gain: *1200 feet*
Type of Bike: *Mountain Bike*

Ride Rating: *Moderate*
Riding Time: *2-3 hours*
Calories Burned: *600*

Terrain

This ride is mostly on unpaved fire roads with some riding on paved roads. There is some hill climbing at the beginning of the ride and also at the end.

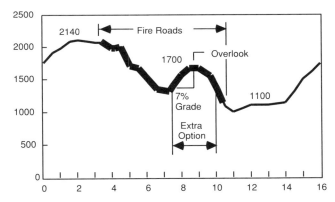

Ride Description

Big Basin Redwoods State Park is the home of some of the most majestic redwoods in the state and has long been enjoyed by South Bay Area residents for its extensive hiking, camping, and picnicking. The 15,000-acre park is located on the western slope of the Santa Cruz Mountains and extend all the way to the sea, at Waddell Creek. Logging was done in the park until about 1902, when the area was established as the California Redwood Park. Today, you can see the stumps of many of the original redwoods surrounded by the second-growth trees, which are rapidly reclaiming the land.

This ride takes you around the eastern end of the park. You start about 3 miles northeast of the park headquarters and begin by climbing up North China Grade, a paved road, to get to Middle Ridge Fire Trail, a rear entrance into the park. This fire road takes you generally downhill into the heart of the park, to the Opal Creek Flatlands, and loops around to the park headquarters. This is a good place to stop and explore the Nature Lodge located there and to hike around through the largest redwood groves in the park. Conclude the ride by continuing north along Opal Creek, on the paved road through the park, and finish by taking the main road (Highway 236) for the last mile back to your car.

This ride is good any time of year, except for the coldest winter days, but is especially good in the spring, when the creeks are flowing, and in the summer, when the cool shade of the mighty redwood trees provides comfort and tranquility.

Starting Point

Big Basin Redwoods State Park is located over the hill from Saratoga. To get there, take Big Basin Way (Highway 9) through Saratoga. It becomes Congress Springs Road after it leaves town and climbs to cross Skyline Blvd at the top. Continue across Skyline Blvd for about 6 miles to the intersection with Highway 236. Turn right onto Highway 236 and proceed for about 5 miles to the intersection with China Grade. Park near this intersection to begin the ride.

Ride Details and Mile Markers

0.0   Begin the ride by going up the hill on North China Grade.

0.7   Flat section.

2.4   Continue straight at the intersection, there is a road on the right. The dirt road begins.

3.3   Turn left onto Middle Ridge Fire Road and begin downhill.

4.1   Turn left to stay on Middle Ridge Fire Road.

4.2   Gate.

6.2   Continue straight to stay on Middle Ridge Fire Road.

6.6   Turn right onto Gazos Creek Road and then immediately turn left to get back onto Middle Ridge Fire Road.

6.8   Steep uphill section.

7.0   Steep uphill section.

7.4   Turn left onto Hihn Hammond Road and begin downhill section. [**Option:** Turn right to Overlook].

7.7   Trail junction on right.

7.9   Turn left onto paved path (Hihn Hammond Road).

8.0   Cross bridge.

8.2   Go over the gate, then turn left at the path split.

8.6   Turn left into the park at Park Headquarters, on the right.

8.7   Store and gift shop are on the right.

8.9   Continue straight at road intersection on left side.

9.8   Gate — road narrows to bike path.

10.0 Bridge.

11.1 Bridge — then begin climb.

12.2 End of bike path at gate — turn left onto road (Highway 236).

13.3 End of ride.

Extra Option (1.2 miles)

There is an extra option in this ride at the 7.4-mile mark. This option will take you about 1.2 miles uphill with an elevation gain of about 300 feet to a overlook point. At the overlook, you will get a panoramic view of the entire Waddell Creek Basin, extending all the way to the sea, about 5 miles away. To ride this Option, turn right on the Hihn Hammond Road, instead of left. Follow the trail uphill to the overlook, which is impossible to miss. Return the way you came to resume your ride at the 7.4-mile mark.

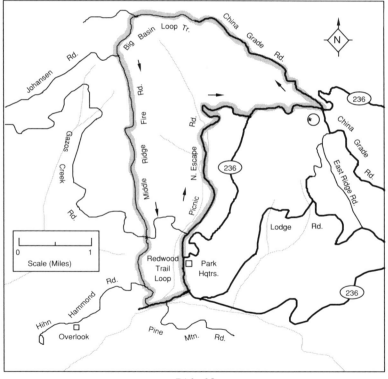

Ride 19

South County:
Ranches and Farms

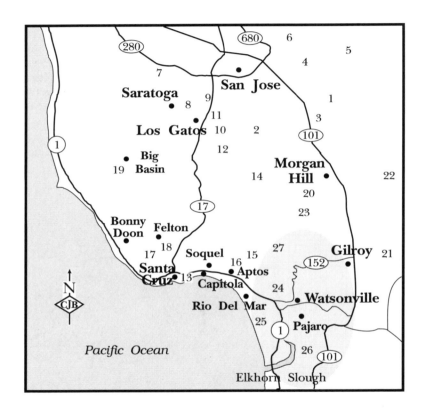

20 **MORGAN HILL**
Chesbro and Uvas Reservoirs

Region: *South County*
Total Distance: *15 miles*
Total Elevation Gain: *500 feet*
Type of Bike: *Road Bike*

Ride Rating: *Moderate*
Riding Time: *2 hours*
Calories Burned: *400*

Terrain
There are no serious hills along the route, and the roads usually carry very little traffic. There are very few services available along the ride, so you might want to bring a snack along with you.

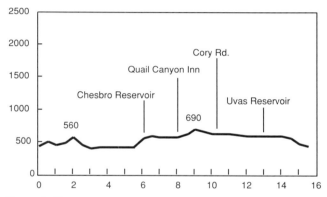

Ride Description
Martin Murphy was the patriarch of a large Irish family that settled in the area in 1844. His son, Daniel Murphy, eventually came to own a vast amount of land, some 10,000 acres. Daniel's land manager and brother-in-law, one Hiram Morgan Hill, supplied the name for the town, Morgan Hill.

This ride completes a loop around Chesbro and Uvas (Spanish for "Grapes") Reservoirs in the rural countryside in the hills west of the town of Morgan Hill.

The ride is good any time of year, although it is best in the spring when the hillsides are green.

Starting Point
You can start this ride anywhere along the route, but if you start at the intersection of Watsonville Road and Uvas Road, the Sycamore Creek Winery can serve as a nice place to relax and taste some wine

before you head home. There are some parking spots on Watsonville Road which are easy to find.

To get there, take the Tennant Avenue exit from Highway 101 at Morgan Hill and proceed west on Tennant to Monterey Road. Turn left onto Monterey Road and then turn right onto Watsonville Road. The Uvas Road intersection is about 3.6 miles west of Monterey Road.

Ride Details and Mile Markers

0.0 Go east on Watsonville Road (toward Morgan Hill). This is a busy road, so watch for traffic and ride carefully.

0.6 Turn left onto Sycamore Avenue.

2.7 Turn left onto Oak Glen Avenue.

3.7 Intersection with Edmundson Avenue is on the right.

5.2 Bear right sharply as Chesbro Road intersects on the left.

5.4 Turn left at the stop sign to stay on Oak Glen. Llagas Road intersects on the right.

5.8 Chesbro Reservoir is visible off to the left.

6.8 Willow Springs Road intersection is on the right.

7.8 Quail Canyon Inn is on the left.

8.5 Turn left onto Uvas Road.

10.1 Little Uvas Road is on the right.

10.3 Intersection with Cory Road is on the right. Uvas Canyon County Park is at the end of Cory Road, about 4 miles away. Hiking trails, a picnic area, and restrooms are all available at the park. Bikes are not permitted on the trails. If you brought a snack, this is a good place to stop. The ride to the park is slightly uphill and goes along a lightly travelled country road. There is no other outlet, so you must return on this road.

13.0 Uvas Reservoir is off to the left.

14.7 Campground is on the right.

15.2 Sycamore Creek Winery is on the right has a tasting room and a gazebo that overlooks the vineyards. You are almost back at your starting point, so this is a good opportunity to taste some of the fine wines available here.

15.3 Back to Watsonville Road.

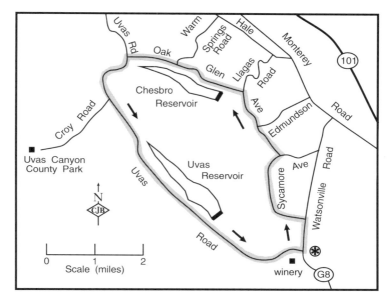

Ride 20

Wine-tasting at Sycamore Creek Winery

Photo: Conrad J. Boisvert

21 GILROY
Gilroy Hot Springs and Cañada Road

Region: *South County*
Total Distance: *23 miles*
Total Elevation Gain: *1000 feet*
Type of Bike: *Road Bike*

Ride Rating: *Moderate*
Riding Time: *2-3 hours*
Calories Burned: *700*

Terrain

The majority of the ride is over country roads with one steady hill climb. The ride is good any time of year, although it is best in the spring, when the hills are green.

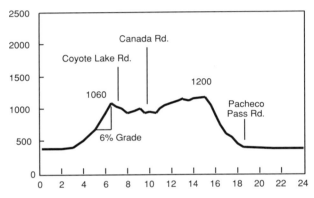

Ride Description

The city of Gilroy was originally named in honor of one of its early residents, John Gilroy. A soapmaker and millwright by trade, Gilroy's main claim to fame seems to have been his marriage to the daughter of Ygnacio Ortega, the owner of Rancho San Ysidro, a 4460-acre property. Gilroy became owner of part of the rancho when Ygnacio died in 1833; however, he ultimately died in poverty at the age of 73 in 1869. His true character may be revealed by the fact that his real name was Cameron, and he only took the name Gilroy, his mother's maiden name, to avoid capture after jumping ship in Monterey in 1814.

This ride starts in Gilroy and follows beautiful remote country roads east of town and up into the hills. Gilroy Hot Springs Road and Cañada Road meander through wooded ranch lands with little or no traffic to contend with. There is a hill climb of about 700 feet to get up to these roads, but then they follow a generally flat to rolling terrain until coming back around and dropping down again into Gilroy.

Leave town heading directly east on 6th Street and Gilman Road. Holsclaw Road takes you to Leavesley Road, and then to New Avenue. Roop Road finally gets you off the main roads and into the country as it climbs toward Coyote Lake County Park, where it then meets with Gilroy Hot Springs Road for the loop around through the country above Gilroy. Cañada Road continues around the loop and eventually comes down to meet with Pacheco Pass Road (Highway 152) and back to town.

Starting Point

To get to Gilroy, head south on Highway 101 and get off at the Leavesley Road exit for Gilroy. Turn right on Leavesley Road for the short distance to Monterey Street in town. Turn left and look for the intersection with 6th Street. Park anywhere around this area.

Ride Details and Mile Markers

0.0   Proceed east on 6th Street from Monterey Street in Gilroy.

0.5   Cross Highway 101. 6th Street becomes Gilman Road.

1.6   Cross the creek and turn left onto Holsclaw Road.

2.8   Turn right onto Leavesley Road.

3.2   Turn left onto New Avenue.

3.7   Turn right onto Roop Road.

5.7   Leavesley Road intersection is on the right.

6.3   End of climb.

7.0   Coyote Lake Road intersection of the left. Road changes name to Gilroy Hot Springs Road.

9.7   Turn right onto Cañada Road. Gilroy Hot Springs Road continues ahead for about 2.6 miles to its end.

12.7   Jamison Road intersection is on the left. Jamison Road goes for about 1.8 miles until it ends.

14.7   Begin descent.

18.5   Turn right onto Pacheco Pass Road (Highway 152).

18.7   Turn left to stay on Pacheco Pass Road.

20.3   Turn right onto Holsclaw Road.

21.7   Turn left onto Gilman Road.

22.8   Cross Highway 101 and begin 6th Street.

23.3   End of ride on Monterey Street.

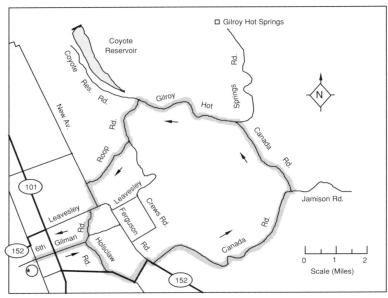

Ride 21

Windmill along Cañada Road

22 MORGAN HILL
Henry Coe State Park

	Ride 22A	Ride 22B
Region:	South County	South County
Ride Rating:	Moderate	Difficult
Total Distance:	5.5 miles	10 miles
Riding Time:	2 hours	3-4 hours
Total Elevation Gain:	800 feet	2100 feet
Calories Burned:	300	800
Type of Ride:	Mountain	Mountain

Terrain

The terrain is a constantly rolling one, with many steep uphill climbs. In addition, part of the trail is a very steep downhill on a very narrow, single-track trail. Because of the extreme heat and dryness in the summer months, it is best to take this ride in the spring or late fall.

Ride Description

The former Coe Ranch, just east of Morgan Hill, is the present Henry Coe State Park, encompassing approximately 67,000 acres, 22,000 of which are maintained as a wilderness area. The ranch was homesteaded in 1883 by the Coe brothers, Henry and Charles. Ultimately, Henry bought out his brother, and over the years continued to acquire more land as other homesteaders in the area left to search for more hospitable land.

Henry's daughter, Sada Coe Robinson, continued to operate the ranch after her father's death. In 1953, she gave the property to the "people of California," as a memorial to her father and, in 1958, it became part of the California State Park System.

These rides cover only a small portion of the park, but will provide adequate challenge and variety to all but the most advanced riders.

Starting Point

To get to Henry Coe State Park, head south from San Jose on Highway 101 to Morgan Hill. Get off at East Dunne Avenue and head east. Climb and wind your way for about 12 miles to the park.

Ride 22A (Moderate)

This ride will take you east from park headquarters on the main fire road, climbing about 200 feet and then descending about 600 feet to the

Manzanita Point Group Camp. Return to park headquarters by reversing your route, for a total distance of around 5.5 miles.

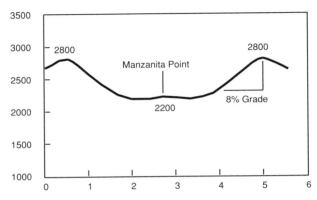

Ride 22A: Ride Details and Mile Markers

0.0 Get on the fire road across from the Visitor Center and begin climbing.

0.5 Continue straight ahead at the junction of the fire trail with the monument on the left.

1.7 Bear right at the split in the fire road, heading toward Manzanita Point Group Camp.

2.4 Bear left at the trail split, heading toward China Hole.

2.7 Turn around and return the way you came.

5.5 End of ride, at park headquarters.

Ride 22B (Difficult)

This ride starts on the main fire trail through the park and climbs immediately to the monument to Henry Coe. Continuing downhill past Frog Lake, climb again and get off the fire road for a long stretch on the single-track Middle Ridge Trail. After a short climb, this trail takes you down a long and sometimes very treacherous 1600-foot descent to the merging of the Middle and Little Forks of Coyote Creek. The growth is very dense in this area and you should expect to walk your bike through some of the most difficult parts. After crossing the creek, return to park headquarters on the fire road, climbing very steeply, with an elevation gain of about 1400 feet.

Ride 22B: Ride Details and Mile Markers

0.0 Get on the fire road across the road from the Visitor Center and begin climbing.

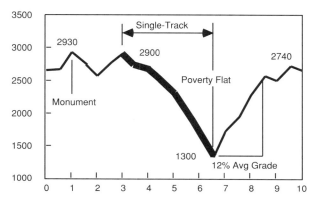

0.5 Turn left at the junction of two fire roads and climb toward the monument.

0.6 Steep uphill section.

1.0 Summit.

1.6 Bear left to stay on the fire road at the trailhead for Frog Lake.

2.0 Climb.

2.2 Frog Lake is to the right.

2.7 Summit — downhill section.

3.0 Turn right at summit — head toward Frog Lake on single-track trail.

3.2 Bear left at trail junction — Frog Lake trail goes off to the right.

3.3 Downhill section.

3.7 Bottom — climb for a bit.

4.0 Summit — descend for 2.5 miles — very steep, narrow, and treacherous.

4.4 Bear left at trail split to head toward Poverty Flat.

5.0 Very steep downhill section — walk your bike.

6.4 Cross over the stream.

6.5 Cross over the stream and turn right onto the fire road — begin climbing.

8.1 Go straight at junction with fire road on the left.

9.8 End of ride, back at park headquarters.

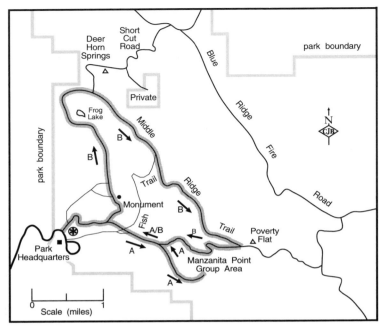

Rides 22A and 22B

Buildings at the old Coe Ranch

23 MORGAN HILL
Mount Madonna Hill Climb

Region: *South County*
Distance: *15 miles*
Total Elevation Gain: *1500 feet*
Type of Bike: *Road Bike*

Ride Rating: *Moderate*
Riding Time: *2 Hours*
Calories Burned: *700*

Terrain

Although Redwood Retreat Road is flat, Mount Madonna Road climbs about 1400 feet, most of it on an unpaved surface. If you have a mountain bike, use it here; otherwise a road bike will work fine, since the road is relatively smooth for a dirt road.

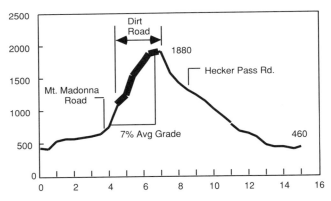

Ride Description

Two little-known, yet marvelously enjoyable rural roads are found just west of Morgan Hill. Redwood Retreat Road and Mount Madonna Road take you to the top of the mountain ridge on this ride, to Mt. Madonna County Park.

At Mt. Madonna County Park, there are hiking and equestrian trails, as well as restrooms. Busy Hecker Pass Road (Highway 152) returns down the hill very quickly to meet Watsonville Road for the return to the starting point.

Both Redwood Retreat Road and Mount Madonna Road have very little traffic, however, Hecker Pass Road is often busy, especially on weekends. The steep downhill on Hecker Pass Road permits you to maintain speeds of about 25-35 mph, enough to very nearly keep up with car traffic, or at least to minimize the amount of time you will be on the road with it.

Starting Point

Start the ride at the intersection of Watsonville Road and Burchell Road, just west of Morgan Hill. There is a small park at this intersection with ample parking. To get there, take the Tennant Avenue exit from Highway 101 at Morgan Hill and proceed west on Tennant to Monterey Road. Turn left onto Monterey Road and then, about ½-mile later, turn right onto Watsonville Road. The Burchell Road intersection is about 5.5 miles west of Monterey Road.

Ride Details and Mile Markers

0.0   From the corner of Watsonville Road and Burchell Road, head west on Watsonville Road.

0.1   Cross the bridge and make a right turn onto Redwood Retreat Road.

2.6   Bridge over the stream.

3.2   Another bridge over the stream.

3.6   Turn left onto Mount Madonna Road and begin climbing.

4.5   Dirt road begins.

6.1   Turn left onto Pole Line Road at the intersection with Summit Road, on the right, and enter Mt. Madonna County Park.

6.5   Deer pen is on the left.

7.0   Summit of ride, about 1880 feet.

7.2   Very steep downhill section — 20% grade over the next 0.2 mile.

8.2   Another steep downhill section.

8.4   Turn left onto Hecker Pass Road (Highway 152).

13.2   Hecker Pass Winery is on the left.

13.3   Fortino Winery is on left.

13.5   Turn left onto Watsonville Road.

14.6   Redwood Retreat Road intersection is on left.

14.8   End of ride, at intersection with Burchell Road.

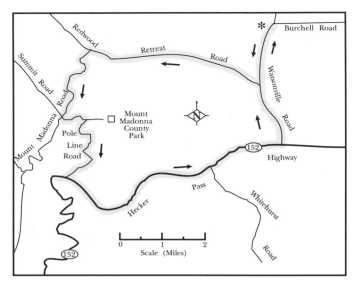

Ride 23

Redwood Retreat Road

Photo: Conrad J. Boisvert

Watsonville Area: Orchards and Farms

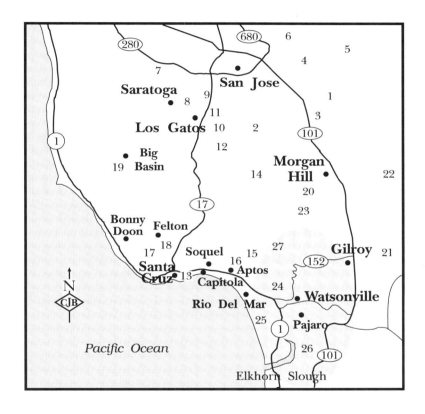

24 CORRALITOS
Corralitos and Green Valley Loop

Region: *Watsonville Area*
Total Distance: *35 miles*
Total Elevation Gain: *1300 feet*
Type of Bike: *Road Bike*

Ride Rating: *Moderate*
Riding Time: *4 hours*
Calories Burned: *1000*

Terrain

There are no serious hill climbs on this ride, but the constant rolling terrain will challenge you just as much. The orchards are especially beautiful in the spring, when the blooms are fullest, but you can enjoy the ride any time of year.

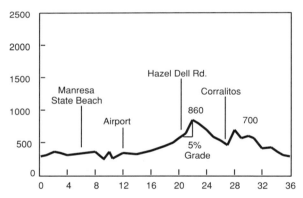

Ride Description

Corralitos is a small farming community located between Santa Cruz and Watsonville. The area around Corralitos is very popular with cyclists. The roads meander over gently rolling hills through strawberry fields, apple orchards and dense forests. The scenic backdrops are Mount Madonna in the east and the Pacific Ocean in the west.

This ride starts in Aptos, just north and west of Corralitos. Head south on Soquel Drive and cross Highway 1 onto Rio Del Mar Blvd. Club House Drive will take you through the quiet residential section of Rio Del Mar. Sumner Avenue and Seascape Blvd will then pass through the community of Seascape. San Andreas Road will take you past Manresa State Beach and the community of La Selva Beach.

Buena Vista Drive crosses Highway 1 once again and past the Watsonville Airport to Freedom Blvd, Airport Blvd, and Green Valley

Road. Green Valley Road wanders through orchards and farmlands as it heads east toward the mountains. At the base of the mountains get on Hazel Dell Road you will ride through thick forests and occasional orchards. Hazel Dell Road becomes Browns Valley Road and leads to Corralitos and its landmark grocery store.

Hames Road, Freedom Blvd., Day Valley Road, and Valencia Road wind through the peaceful countryside and lead you to Trout Gulch Road and the return to Aptos on Soquel Drive.

Starting Point

Start at the Santa Cruz Coffee Roasting Company in Aptos. To get there, go south from Santa Cruz on Highway 1. Get off at the Seacliff Beach-Aptos exit, and turn left onto State Park Drive. Turn right onto Soquel Drive and go into the shopping center on the right (Safeway store). Look for the coffee roasting company store. Arrive a few minutes early and have coffee and a muffin before you begin the ride.

Ride Details and Mile Markers

0.0 Head south on Soquel Drive.

0.3 Cross under the railroad bridge and bear left to stay on Soquel Drive.

0.5 Continue straight at the Trout Gulch Drive intersection.

1.5 Turn right onto Rio Del Mar Blvd and cross over Highway 1.

1.7 Turn left onto Club House Drive.

3.3 Turn left onto Sumner Avenue.

3.8 Turn left onto Seascape Blvd.

4.6 Turn right onto San Andreas Road.

5.4 Cross Playa Blvd. [**Option:** Turn right to explore the community of La Selva.]

6.0 Manresa State Beach is on theright side.

6.8 Sand Dollar Drive is on the right.

7.9 Turn left onto Buena Vista Drive and cross the railroad tracks. [**Option:** Continue straight ahead for about 1 mile to Sunset Beach Road for a side trip to Sunset Beach State Park.]

10.4 Cross under Highway 1.

10.9 Cross Larkin Valley Road — then climb short distance.

11.9 Airport is on the right.

12.7 Turn right onto Freedom Blvd.

12.9 Turn left onto Airport Blvd.

13.2 Pass through orchards.

13.4 Turn left onto Green Valley Road.

15.5 Casserly Road is on the right.

15.9 Pioneer Road is on the left.

16.3 More orchards.

20.5 Turn left onto Hazel Dell Road, which later becomes Browns Valley Road.

26.8 Turn right at the intersection to stay on Browns Valley Road and cross the bridge.

27.0 Corralitos grocery store. This is a good place for a snack. Continue straight to begin Hames Road — climb the hill.

28.5 Road bends to the right and then to the left — stay on Hames Road.

29.2 Turn right onto Freedom Blvd.

29.3 Turn right onto Day Valley Road — climb the hill.

31.3 Turn right onto Valencia Road.

34.0 Turn left onto Trout Gulch Road.

34.5 Turn right onto Soquel Drive.

34.6 [**Option:** Turn right onto Aptos Creek Road to explore the forest of the Nisene Marks State Park. Earthquake epicenter marker is about 5 miles up the trail. The trail is easily accessible on road bikes.]

35.0 End of ride, back at the shopping center.

Orchards along Green Valley Road   Photo: Conrad J. Boisvert

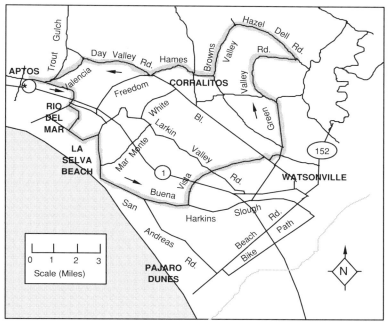

Ride 24

25 RIO DEL MAR
Rio Del Mar — Watsonville Loop

Region: *Watsonville Area*
Total Distance: *24 miles*
Total Elevation Gain: *600 feet*
Type of Bike: *Road Bike*

Ride Rating: *Moderate*
Riding Time: *2-3 hours*
Calories Burned: *600*

Terrain

There are some traffic spots to contend with along the way, but generally, the ride is along country roads with little or no traffic. There are plenty of rolling hills, but no serious climbs.

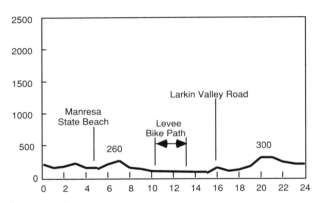

Ride Description

In 1852, Judge John H. Watson and D. S. Gregory laid out the town of Watsonville. The first apple orchard was planted in 1853 and, in the following years, the town would see its reputation as a farming community grow as fast as its fruits and vegetables.

This ride starts in the town of Rio Del Mar and heads south along the coast, past Manresa and Sunset Beaches, to Pajaro Dunes. It then follows the levee along the Pajaro River inland to Watsonville and passes by many of the farms and canning factories that support the local economy.

From Watsonville, the route heads north along Larkin Valley Road through rural countryside and returns to Rio Del Mar.

Starting Point

The starting point for this ride is at the Deer Park Shopping Mall in Rio Del Mar, just off Highway 1. To get there, take Highway 1 south from Santa Cruz to the Rio Del Mar exit at Rio Del Mar Blvd. Turn right onto Rio Del Mar Blvd, then turn right again almost immediately into the shopping center parking area.

Ride Details and Mile Markers

0.0 Start — turn right out of shopping center onto Rio Del Mar Blvd.

0.4 Golf course.

0.5 Turn left onto Sumner Avenue.

1.8 Continue straight through at the Club House Drive intersection.

2.3 Turn left at Seascape Blvd and climb a short hill.

3.1 Turn right onto San Andreas Road.

3.9 Cross the Playa Blvd intersection. La Selva Beach is to the right, if you wish to explore a bit.

4.6 Manresa Beach State Park is on the right side.

5.3 Sand Dollar Drive intersection is on the right side.

6.4 Buena Vista Drive intersection is on the left.

7.7 Road to Sunset Beach State Park is on the right.

8.0 Strawberry fields are on the left.

9.8 Turn left onto Beach Road. Pajaro Dunes Beach is down Beach Road to the right.

9.9 Turn right onto Thurwachter Road to get to the bike path on the levee.

10.2 Turn left on the levee bike path. Farmland is on the left, and the Pajaro River is on the right.

10.6 Water treatment plant is on the left.

11.2 Bike path goes under Highway 1.

12.8 Salamander crossing.

12.9 Gate and railroad tracks. Turn left onto Walker Street.

13.4 Cross Beach Road.

13.8 Beginning of Harkins Slough Road.

14.2 Park, playground and ballfield.

14.9 Turn right onto Green Valley Road.

15.2 Turn left onto Main Street (Highway 152).

15.5 Turn right onto Holm Road, then make immediate left turn onto Westgate Drive.

16.0 Cross over Airport Blvd and begin Larkin Valley Road.

17.2 Cross Buena Vista Road.

19.8 Intersection with Mar Monte Drive is on the left. Continue straight ahead and climb.

20.2 White Road is on the right. Downhill section.

21.4 Road crosses under Highway 1 and becomes San Andreas Road.

21.6 Turn right onto Bonita Drive.

22.8 Intersection with Freedom Blvd is on the left. Continue straight ahead. Road goes through, even though sign indicates it doesn't. Road is unpaved and bumpy.

23.1 Paved section begins.

23.7 Cross over at the Club House Drive intersection.

23.8 End of ride at Deer Park Center.

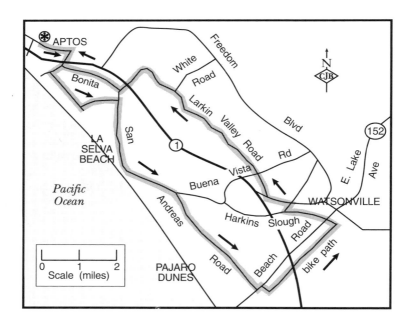

Ride 25

26 PAJARO
Pajaro Valley and the Elkhorn Slough

Region: *Watsonville Area*
Total Distance: *25 miles*
Total Elevation Gain: *700 feet*
Type of Bike: *Road Bike*

Ride Rating: *Moderate*
Riding Time: *3 hours*
Calories Burned: *600*

Terrain

Rolling hills with no major climbs result in this ride being a very relaxing one. Most of the roads have little traffic, except for Castroville Blvd. and San Juan Road, and both of these have adequate shoulders. There are few services available along this route, so pack a snack if you think you might need it.

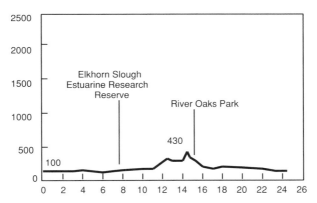

Ride Description

The Elkhorn Slough is one of the few remaining undisturbed wetlands in California and serves as a major link in the Pacific Flyway for migrating birds. It is comprised of about 2500 acres of mudflats and coastal tidelands and supports a very complex ecosystem. The name probably comes from the tule elk that once roamed the area and served as part of the diet of the Ohlone Indians some 10,000 to 15,000 years ago.

On the eastern edge of the slough, the Elkhorn Slough National Estuarine Research Reserve was established in 1979. Comprising 1300 acres, it is used as a research center for this rich and diverse natural treasure. There is a visitor center at the reserve that offers interpretive displays, demonstrating the workings of the slough. Open Wednesday through Sunday, the Reserve also has a raised-relief model of the undersea Monterey Canyon.

The ride starts out in the town of Pajaro (Spanish for "bird") and heads south out of town, along Salinas Road. Elkhorn Road then leads along the eastern side of the Elkhorn Slough, past the visitor center for the Research Reserve, to Castroville Blvd. Head east for a short distance and then north on San Miguel Canyon Road, Echo Valley Road, Maher Road and San Miguel Canyon Road to meet up with San Juan Road for the return to Pajaro.

Starting Point

Start the ride in Pajaro. To get there, head south on Highway 1 from Santa Cruz. Get off at the Riverside Drive (Highway 129) exit and head east to Main Street (Highway G12). Turn right onto Main Street and continue past the intersection with San Juan Road. Main Street becomes Salinas Road. Park anywhere along this road.

An alternate route is from Highway 101, exiting at Highway 129 and heading west toward Pajaro. From this direction, turn left onto Main Street (G12).

Ride Details and Mile Markers

0.0   Head south on Salinas Road.

0.7   Lewis Road intersection is on the left.

1.5   Turn left to get on Elkhorn Road.

2.3   Intersection with Hudson Landing Road is on the right. Cross the bridge.

2.5   Bear right to stay on Elkhorn Road at its intersection with Hall Road, on the left.

4.5   Elkhorn Slough is to the right.

4.8   Kirby Park Access Area is on the right.

6.2   Climb.

7.5   Elkhorn Slough National Estuarine Research Reserve is on the right. Visitor Center is open Wednesday through Sunday, 9 a.m. to 5 p.m.

9.5   Turn left onto Castroville Blvd. Climb steadily.

10.9   Paradise Road os on the left.

12.6   Turn left onto San Miguel Canyon Road.

13.2   Pond Derosa is on right.

13.5   Turn right onto Echo Valley Road.

14.0   Turn left onto Maher Road and climb a short hill.

15.1   Royal Oaks Park is on the right.

17.0 Turn left onto Tarpey Road and then right onto San Miguel Canyon Road.

18.2 Lewis Road is on the left.

19.6 Turn left onto Vega Road. Climb.

21.9 Turn right onto Lewis Road.

24.2 Turn right onto Salinas Road.

24.5 End of ride.

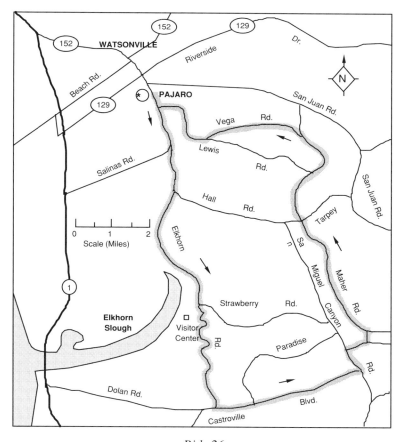

Ride 26

27 CORRALITOS
Corralitos and Summit Road Loop

Region: *Watsonville Area*
Total Distance: *42 miles*
Total Elevation Gain: *3100 feet*
Type of Bike: *Road Bike*

Ride Rating: *Difficult*
Riding Time: *4-5 hours*
Calories Burned: *1600*

Terrain

This is a very difficult ride and should only be undertaken by the strongest riders. It includes over 3000 feet of elevation gain, with some very steep terrain on Mt. Bache Road. Summit Road is unpaved for much of its length.

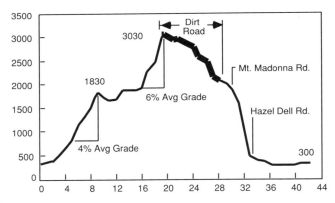

Ride Description

Starting from Corralitos, near Watsonville, the ride goes up Eureka Canyon Road, following Corralitos Creek, past orchards and rustic residential areas. As it progresses up the hill toward Summit Road, there are fewer homes and the thick redwood forest dominates the scene. At the crest of Eureka Canyon Road, the Forest of Nisene Marks State Park comes into view, beyond the valley below.

Mt. Bache Road leads to the top of the mountains and Summit Road. Summit Road, along the crest, is unpaved with a gate across each end of the road, but bikes are permitted on the road. The land along the road is private, however, and every effort should be made to respect the privacy of the residents. Touring bike tires will usually suffice on the dirt of Summit Road, unless there has been a recent rainfall. To compensate for the hard work of the hill climb, there are some spectacular views both east and west from the crest of the coastal mountain range on Summit Road.

Mt. Madonna Road returns to the valley floor. Enjoy the country roads as they meander through orchards and wooded countryside and return to Corralitos.

The ride is good any time of year, except when it is cold or windy, or after a recent rain, when the dirt road can become impassable on a touring bike. It is especially good in the spring, when everything is green and the flowers are blooming.

Starting Point

The little town of Corralitos in Santa Cruz County serves as the starting point for this ride. Corralitos can be reached by taking Highway 1 south from Santa Cruz to the Freedom Blvd exit. Head north on Freedom Blvd and turn left onto Hames Road after about 2.5 miles. Travel 1.5 miles on Hames Road, to arrive at a little grocery store at the intersection of Hames Road, Corralitos Road, Eureka Canyon Road, and Browns Valley Road. This intersection is not as busy as it sounds and parking is easy to find.

Ride Details and Mile Markers

0.0   Start the ride by proceeding north on Eureka Canyon Road out of Corralitos.

2.3   Rider Road intersection is on the left.

4.8   Lower Highland Way intersection is on the left.

5.4   Kononia Conference Center (private) entrance on the left.

6.0   Camp Corralitos (private).

9.3   First summit on Eureka Canyon Road. Downhill begins.

9.4   Eureka Canyon Road becomes Highland Way (not obvious on the road).

9.8   Camp Loma (private).

11.5   Begin climbing again.

15.5   Spanish Ranch Road intersection is on the left.

15.8   Turn right onto Mt. Bache Road. Begin steep climb.

16.8   Loma Prieta Avenue intersection is on the left. Straight ahead is the start of Loma Prieta Road.

17.5   False summit — downhill for a bit.

18.4   Final climb to Summit Road.

19.0   Unpaved road begins.

19.5   Turn right at the road split to get on Summit Road. Summit Road (on the right) is marked by a gate across the road. The road is public, but the property along the road is privately owned.

This road continues unpaved for the next 7 miles, or so. It is mostly downhill, but some uphill sections will be encountered along the way.

27.0 Gate across the road. Paved road begins.

30.5 Turn right onto Mt. Madonna Road for a steep and winding descent to the valley floor.

33.0 Turn right onto Hazel Dell Road at the bottom of the hill.

33.5 Turn left onto Green Valley Road.

38.0 Turn right onto Pioneers Road.

39.5 Pioneers Road becomes Varni Road after crossing Amesti Road.

40.5 Turn right onto Corralitos Road.

42.0 Back at Corralitos store.

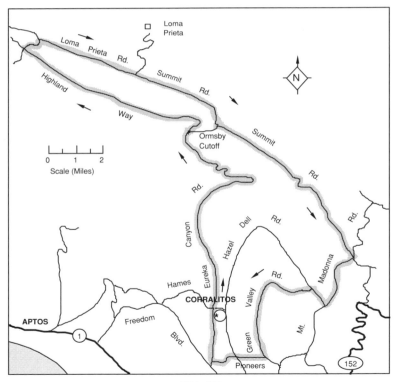

Ride 27

APPENDIX

RIDES BY RATINGS

Easy Rides
(short rides, easy grades, for beginners and children)

3. Coyote Creek Bike Path (14 miles) 17
6. Alum Rock Park (9 miles) 27
8. Los Gatos, Villa Montalvo, and Saratoga (13 miles) 34
9. Los Gatos Creek Trail (13 miles) 37
13. Santa Cruz and Capitola Beach Ride (23 miles) 55
14A. Along the Crest of Summit Road (7 miles) 58
16A. Forest of Nisene Marks State Park (10 miles) 66
18. Henry Cowell Redwoods State Park (8 miles) 78

Moderate Rides
(longer rides, some hills, not too strenuous)

1. San Felipe Valley (22 miles) 11
2. New Almaden and Hicks Road Hill Climb (20 miles) 14
5. Grant Ranch County Park (10 miles) 23
7. Saratoga and Stevens Canyon Back Roads (14.5 miles) 31
10B. Sierra Azul Open Space Preserve (10 miles) 44
11. St. Joseph's Hill Open Space Preserve (6 miles) 46
16B. Forest of Nisene Marks State Park (22 miles) 68
17A. Empire Grade and Bonny Doon Loop (27 miles) 73
17B. Empire Grade and Bonny Doon Loop (32 miles) 75
19. Big Basin Redwoods State Park (13 miles) 81
20. Chesbro and Uvas Reservoirs (15 miles) 85
21. Gilroy Hot Springs and Cañada Road (23 miles) 88
22A. Henry Coe State Park (5.5 miles) 91
23. Mount Madonna Hill Climb (15 miles) 96
24. Corralitos and Green Valley Loop (35 miles) 100
25. Rio Del Mar — Watsonville Loop (24 miles) 104
26. Pajaro Valley and the Elkhorn Slough (25 miles) 107

Difficult Rides
(extensive rides with strenuous grades, for more experienced cyclists)

4. Quimby Road Loop (18 miles) 20
10A. Sierra Azul Open Space Preserve (12 miles) 41
12. Mountain Charlie Road (50 miles) 51
14B. Along the Crest of Summit Road (37 miles) 59
15. Eureka Canyon and Soquel Loop (40 miles) 62
16C. Forest of Nisene Marks State Park (31 miles) 70
22B. Henry Coe State Park (10 miles) 92
27. Corralitos and Summit Road Loop (42 miles) 110

MOUNTAIN BIKE RIDES

5. Grant Ranch County Park (Moderate) 23
6. Alum Rock Park (Easy) 27
10A. Sierra Azul Open Space Preserve (Difficult) 41
10B. Sierra Azul Open Space Preserve (Moderate) 44
11. St. Joseph's Hill Open Space Preserve (Moderate) 46
16A. Forest of Nisene Marks (Easy)) 66
16B. Forest of Nisene Marks (Moderate) 68
16C. Forest of Nisene Marks (Difficult) 70
18. Henry Cowell Redwoods State Park (Easy) 78
19. Big Basin Redwoods State Park (Moderate) 81
22A. Henry Coe State Park (Moderate) 91
22B. Henry Coe State Park (Difficult) 92

The Elkhorn Slough

Photo: Conrad J. Boisvert

BICYCLE SHOPS IN THE SOUTH BAY

Aptos

Bicycle Inn
6195 Soquel Dr.
Aptos, CA 95003
(408) 476-0928

Mike's Bikes II
7960-A Soquel Dr.
Aptos, CA 95003
(408) 688-8650

Campbell

Wheel Away Cycle Center
402 E. Hamilton Ave.
Campbell, CA 95008
(408) 378-4636

Cupertino

Any Mountain
10495 N. De Anza Blvd.
Cupertino, CA 95014
(408) 255-6162

Cupertino Bike Shop
21670 Stevens Creek
Blvd.
Cupertino, CA 95014
(408) 255-2217

Mike's Bikes
10883 S. Blaney Ave
Cupertino, CA 95014
(408) 253-6940

REI
20640 Homestead Rd.
Cupertino, CA 95014
(408) 446-1991

Stan's Bicycle Store
19685 Stevens Creek
Blvd.
Cupertino, CA 95014
(408) 966-1234

Gilroy

Sunshine Bicycles
309 First St.
Gilroy, CA 95020
(408) 842-4889

Los Gatos

Kennedy's Cycles
1454 Pollard Rd.
Los Gatos, CA 95030
(408) 379-9810

Los Gatos Schwinn Cyclery
15954 Los Gatos Blvd.
Los Gatos, CA 95030
(408) 356-1644

Mr. Hills Bicycles
15724 Los Gatos Blvd.
Los Gatos, CA 95030
(408) 356-4644

Velomeister Fine Cycles
104 University Ave.
Los Gatos, CA 95030
(408) 395-5105

Milpitas

*Paramount Cyclery &
Sport Shop*
12 North Abel St.
Milpitas, CA 95035
(408) 945-6580

Spectrum Cycles
1402 Dempsey Rd.
Milpitas, CA 95035
(408) 946-3746

Town & Country Bicycles
1257 Jacklin Rd.
Milpitas, CA 95035
(408) 946-8501

Morgan Hill

Morgan Hill Bike Shop
16825 Monterey Rd.
Morgan Hill, CA 95037
(408) 779-4015

South Valley Bikes
17395 Monterey Rd.
Morgan Hill, CA 95037
(408) 778-6100

Rio Del Mar

Rheads Sports
714 Clubhouse Dr.
Rio Del Mar, CA 95003
(408) 685-9215

San Jose

Bicycles Et Cetera
5965 Almaden Expwy.
San Jose, CA 95120
(408) 997-9147

The Bike Chain
2964 Aborn Square Rd.
San Jose, CA 95121
(408) 274-2919

Bike Works
14910 Camden Ave.
San Jose, CA 95124
(408) 371-7967

Britton's Almaden
6910 Almaden Expwy.
San Jose, CA 95120
(408) 268-6966

Desimone's Cycles
83 South 2nd St.
San Jose, CA 95113
(408) 293-5808

Faber's Cyclery
702 South 1st St.
San Jose, CA 95112
(408) 294-1314

Fast Bicycle
2274 Alum Rock Ave.
San Jose, CA 95116
(408) 251-9110

Fast Bike
1659 Branham Lane
San Jose, CA 95118
(408) 448-6605

Foxworthy Bike Shop
1515 Meridian Ave.
San Jose, CA 95125
(408) 269-2300

Grand Delta Corporation
1250 Yard Ct.
San Jose, CA 95133
(408) 292-5962

Pedalers Hub
1150 Saratoga Ave.
San Jose, CA 95129
(408) 244-7878

San Jose Schwinn
2061 Lincoln Avenue
San Jose, CA 95125
(408) 987-8770

Santa Teresa Bikes
5671 Snell Ave.
San Jose, CA 95123
(408) 226-6080

Slough's Bike Shop
260 Race St.
San Jose, CA 95126
(408) 293-1616

Spartan Bicycles
18B South 8th St.
San Jose, CA 95112
(408) 293-7925

Sunrise Schwinn Cyclery
656 Blossom Hill Rd.
San Jose, CA 95123
(408) 225-4330

Willow Glen Bicycles
1110 Willow St.
San Jose, CA 95125
(408) 293-2606

Santa Clara

Desimone's Cycles
2236 El Camino Real
Santa Clara, CA 95051
(408) 248-8747

Moby Dick Bike Shop
2636 Homestead Rd.
Santa Clara, CA 95051
(408) 246-2777

The Off-Ramp
2369 El Camino Real
Santa Clara, CA 95051
(408) 249-2848

Shaw's Lightweight Cycles
39 Washington St.
Santa Clara, CA 95050
(408) 246-7881

Santa Cruz

Another Bike Shop
1325 Mission St.
Santa Cruz, CA 95060
(408) 427-2232

Bicycle Center
1420 Mission St.
Santa Cruz, CA 95060
(408) 423-6324

The Bicycle Trip
1201 Soquel Ave.
Santa Cruz, CA 95062
(408) 427-2580

Branciforte Bicycle Shop
911 Water St.
Santa Cruz, CA 95062
(408) 426-7299

Dutchman Bicycles
3961 Portola Dr.
Santa Cruz, CA 95062
(408) 476-9555

Flyworks
1829 Soquel Ave.
Santa Cruz, CA 95062
(408) 429-8528

Pacific Ave. Cycles
709 Pacific Ave.
Santa Cruz, CA 95060
(408) 423-1314

Santa Cruz Cyclery
1018 Water St.
Santa Cruz, CA 95062
(408) 429-5951

Santa Cruz Cycling Center
860 41st Ave.
Santa Cruz, CA 95062
(408) 475-3883

Spokesman Bicycles
231 Cathcart
Santa Cruz, CA 95060
(408) 429-6062

Saratoga

Spectrum Cycles
18802 Cox Ave.
Saratoga, CA 95070
(408) 374-5830

Scotts Valley

Scotts Valley Cyclery
3111 Scotts Valley Dr.
Scotts Valley, CA 95066
(408) 438-4777

Sunnyvale

Aardvark Bicycles
1111 W. El Camino Real
Sunnyvale, CA 94087
(408) 733-0263

Spectrum Cycles
1637 Hollenbeck Ave.
Sunnyvale, CA 94087
(408) 737-7333

Walt's Cycle
116 Carroll St.
Sunnyvale, CA 94086
(408) 736-2630

Watsonville

Green Valley Cyclery
1994 Main St.
Watsonville, CA 95076
(408) 722-8171

Mike's Bikes
426 Main St.
Watsonville, CA 95076
(408) 722-8650

*Watsonville Cyclery
& Sports*
202 East Lake Ave.
Watsonville, CA 95076
(408) 728-1166

CYCLING CLUBS IN THE SOUTH BAY

Almaden Cycle Touring Club
Box 7286, San Jose 95150
(408) 997-9737
Recreational cycling and touring.

American Youth Hostels
Central California Council
Box 28148, San Jose 95159
(408) 298-0670
Recreational cycling using hostels.

Bay Area Roaming Tandems (BART)
Box 2176, Los Gatos 95031
(408) 356-7443
Tandems only.

Garden City Cyclists
c/o Shaw's Cycles
39 Washington Street
Santa Clara 95050
(408) 246-7881
Racing, track and instructional rides
for all levels.

Hellyer Park Velodrome Association
Box 7385, San Jose 95150
(408) 295-9257
Race promotions, development and
training.

Los Gatos Bicycle Racing Club
Box 2842, Saratoga 95070
(408) 997-0381
USCF racing and training.

Milpitas Cyclists
(408) 262-2109
Weekly Sunday rides, moderately
fast-paced.

Monterey Mountain Bike Association
(MoMBA)
Box 51923, Pacific Grove 93950
Recreational off-road riding for all
levels.

*Responsible Organized Mountain
Pedalers* (ROMP), Los Gatos
(415) 949-3137
Off-road training and recreational
rides, and activist efforts.

San Jose Bicycle Club
610 So. 12th St., San Jose 95112
(408) 287-7522
USCF racing.

San Jose State University Cyclling Club
(408) 292-2511
Collegiate racing and training.

Santa Clara Valley Bicycle Association
Box 831, Cupertino 95015
(415) 651-6472
Advocacy group.

Santa Cruz County Cycling Club
414½ Soquel Avenue
Santa Cruz 95062
(408) 423-0829
Touring, racing, commuting, safety
and cyclists' rights.

*Santa Cruz County Transportation
Commission Bicycle Committee*
701 Ocean Street, Room 420
Santa Cruz 95060
(408) 425-2951
Advises transportation commission
and local jurisdictions.

Skyline Cycling Club
Box 60176, Sunnyvale 94088
(408) 739-3995
Touring club, some off-road rides.

South Valley Tri-Sports Club
470 Corte Cabanil
Morgan Hill 95037
(408) 778-3713
Competitive cycling, running and
swimming.

Sunnyvale Competitive Cycling Club
Box 245, Cupertino 95015
(408) 733-4087
Training rides for all levels.

Velo Club Monterey
Box 1404, Monterey 93940
(408) 373-0317
USCF racing, recreational touring and
social.

ANNUAL CYCLING EVENTS

Recreational Rides

TIERRA BELLA CENTURY, Gilroy
  Time of year: 1st or 2nd Saturday in April
  Sponsor: Almaden Cycle Touring Club
         P.O. Box 7286, San Jose 95150
         (408) 997-9737

STEINBECK CENTURY, Salinas
  Time of year: April
  Sponsor: Multiple Sclerosis Community Services
         546 Abbott St., #11, Salinas 93901
         (408) 758-1663

MOUNT HAMILTON CHALLENGE AND ASCENT, San Jose
  Time of year: April
  Sponsor: Pedalera Bicycle Club
         P.O. Box 60906, Sunnyvale 94088
         (408) 756-6514

TOUR DE GARLIQUE, Gilroy
  Time of year: July (Sunday of Garlic Festival weekend)
  Sponsor: Gilroy Garlic Festival
         P.O. Box 2311, Gilroy 95021-2311
         (408) 842-1625

PAJARO VALLEY CENTURY, Corralitos
  Time of year: July
  Sponsor: Santa Cruz County Cycling Club
         414½ Soquel Ave., Santa Cruz 95062
         (408) 423-0829

Competitive Racing

CAT'S HILL CRITERIUM, Los Gatos
  Time of year: May
  Sponsor: Los Gatos Bicycle Racing Club
         P.O. Box 2842, Saratoga 95070
         (408) 997-0381

CAPITOLA CRITERIUM, Capitola
  Time of year: April
  Sponsor: Santa Cruz County Cycling Club
         414½ Soquel Ave., Santa Cruz 95062
         (408) 423-0829

QUICKSILVER MOUNTAIN BIKE RACE & TOUR, San Jose
  Time of year: June
  Sponsor: Quickersilver Mountain Bike Race & Tour
         P.O. Box DF, Los Gatos 95031

FAIRS AND EVENTS IN THE SOUTH BAY

Gilroy

Chamber of Commerce:
(408) 842-6437

Gilroy Garlic Festival
Time of year: July

Los Gatos

Chamber of Commerce:
(408) 354-9300

Ming Quong Strawberry
Festival
Time of year: 1st weekend
in June

Summer Fest
(Arts, wine tasting, music)
Time of year: Mid-June

Fiesta Day Arts
(Arts, wine tasting, music)
Time of year: August

Taste of Los Gatos Food
Festival
Time of year: October

Morgan Hill

Chamber of Commerce:
(408) 779-9444

Mushroom Mardi Gras
Time of year: May

San Jose

Chamber of Commerce:
(408) 998-7000

Santa Clara County Fair
Time of year: August

Santa Cruz

Visitors Council:
(408) 425-1234

Natural Bridges Migration
Festival
Time of year: February

Clam Chowder Cook-Off
Time of year: February

Rhododendron Show
Time of year: May

Santa Cruz County Vintners
Festival
Time of year: June

Santa Cruz County Fair
Time of year: September

Annual Santa Cruz Chili
Cook-Off
Time of year: September

Saratoga

Chamber of Commerce:
(408) 867-0753

Easter Promenade
Time of year: Easter Sunday

Saratoga Blossom Festival
Time of year: May

Watsonville

Visitor Council:
(408) 425-1234

West Coast Antique Fly-In Air
Show
Time of year: May

Annual Strawberry Festival
Time of year: June

POINTS OF INTEREST

State Parks

Big Basin Redwoods State Park
Highway 235, Big Basin
(408) 338-6132
Hiking, camping and
mountain biking

Henry W. Coe State Park
East end of East Dunne Ave.
Morgan Hill
(408) 779-2728
Hiking, camping and
mountain biking

Cowell Redwoods State Park
Highway 9, Felton
(408) 335-4598
Hiking, camping and
mountain biking

The Forest of Nisene Marks State Park
Soquel Dr., Aptos
(408) 335-4598
Hiking, camping and
mountain biking

Natural Bridges State Beach
Swanton Blvd., Santa Cruz
(408) 423-4609
Winter home of Monarch
butterflies
(October-February)

Wilder Ranch State Park
Highway 1, North of Santa
Cruz
(408) 688-3421

Santa Clara County Parks

*c/o Santa Clara County Parks
and Recreation
298 Garden Hills Dr.
Los Gatos 95030
(408) 358-3741*

*Almaden Quicksilver County
Park*
Almaden Rd., San Jose
Hiking, picnicking and
equestrians

Alum Rock Park
16240 Alum Rock Ave.
San Jose
(408) 259-5477
Hiking and picnicking

Coyote Creek Parkway
Hellyer Park, Hellyer Ave.
San Jose
Running, walking and biking

Joseph D. Grant County Park
Mount Hamilton Rd., San
Jose
Hiking, picnicking, mountain
biking and equestrians

Mount Madonna County Park
Pole Line Rd., Morgan Hill
(408) 358-3741
Hiking, picnicking, mountain
biking and equestrians

Uvas Canyon County Park
Croy Rd., Morgan Hill
(408) 779-9232
Hiking and picnicking

Villa Montalvo Arboretum
15400 Montalvo Rd.,
Saratoga
(408) 741-3421
Art gallery, hiking trails,
arboretum and docent tours

Museums

Los Gatos Museum
Main St. and Tait Ave.
Los Gatos
(408) 354-2646
Regional historic museum

*Quicksilver County Park
Mining Museum*
21570 New Almaden Rd.
San Jose
(408) 268-1729
Regional historic museum

Santa Cruz Museum of Natural
    History
    1305 E. Cliff Dr., Santa Cruz
    (408) 429-3773
    Regional natural history
    museum, specializing in the
    Northern Monterey Bay area

Wagons to Wings Museum at
    Hill Country
    15060 Foothill Ave.
    Morgan Hill
    (408) 227-4607
    Antique cars and airplanes

Selected Wineries

Bargetto Winery
    3535 N. Main St., Soquel
    (408) 475-2258

Bonny Doon Vineyard
    10 Pine Flat Rd., Santa Cruz
    (408) 425-3625

David Bruce Winery
    21439 Bear Creek Rd.
    Los Gatos
    (408) 395-9548

Congress Springs Vineyards
    23600 Congress Springs Rd.,
    Saratoga
    (408) 741-5424

Fortino Winery
    4525 Hecker Pass Rd., Gilroy
    (408) 842-3305

Hallcrest Vineyards
    379 Felton Empire Rd.,
    Felton
    (408) 335-4441

Hecker Pass Winery
    4605 Hecker Pass Rd., Gilroy
    (408) 842-8755

Kirigin Cellars
    11550 Watsonville Rd.,
    Gilroy
    (408) 847-8827

J. Lohr Winery
    1000 Lenzen Ave., San Jose
    (408) 288-5057

Mirassou Vineyards
    3000 Aborn Rd., San Jose
    (408) 274-4000

Ridge Vineyards
    17100 Montebello Rd.,
    Cupertino
    (408) 867-3723

Sunrise Winery
    13100 Montebello Rd.,
    Cupertino
    (408) 741-1310

Sycamore Creek Winery
    12775 Uvas Rd., Morgan Hill
    (408) 779-4738

Miscellaneous

Elkhorn Slough National
    Estuarine Research Reserve
    1700 Elkhorn Rd.,
    Watsonville
    (408) 728-2822
    Hiking, bird-watching and
    learning center

Opry House at Club Almaden
    21350 Almaden Rd., San Jose
    (408) 268-2492
    Historic restaurant and
    melodrama theater

Roaring Camp & Big Trees
    Narrow Gauge Railroad
    Graham Hill Road & Roaring
    Camp Rd., Felton
    (408) 335-4400
    Steam train rides, picnicking
    and hiking

Santa Cruz Boardwalk and
    Wharf
    Beach Street, Santa Cruz
    Amusement park, deep-sea
    fishing, shops and restaurants

CALIFORNIA BICYCLE LAWS

Excerpted from the 1987 California Vehicle Code, the following descriptions explain laws which pertain to cyclists.

RIGHTS AND RESPONSIBILITIES   21200

A. Bicyclists must obey all the laws which apply to operators of motor vehicles.
B. You must never ride under the influence of alcohol or drugs.

EQUIPMENT REQUIREMENTS   21201

A. You must have operating brakes.
B. Handlebars must not be elevated above the shoulders.
C. The size of the bicycle must not be so large that the operator cannot support the bike in an upright position with at least one foot on the ground.
D. When riding at night, the bicycle must be equipped with a front light, a rear reflector, pedal reflectors, and reflectors visible from the sides, at the front of the bike.

OPERATION ON ROADWAY   21202

A. You must ride as far to the right of the roadway unless you are passing another vehicle, making a left turn, or avoiding hazardous road conditions.
B. On a one-way street, you may ride on the left side if you are as far to the left as practical.

HITCHING RIDES   21203

No person riding a bicycle is permitted to attach the bike or himself to any moving vehicle.

RIDING ON BICYCLE   21204

A. Bike must be equipped with a permanent and upright seat.
B. You may not ride as a passenger unless the bike is equipped with a separate seat. Seats for children must have adequate means of holding the child in place and for protection from moving parts on the bike.
C. Children riding as passengers must wear an ANSI-approved helmet.

CARRYING ARTICLES   21205

You must be able to have at least one hand on the handlebars when carrying an object.

BICYCLE LANES   21208

   A. You must ride in designated bicycle lanes unless you are passing another vehicle in the lane, making a left turn, or avoiding hazardous obstacles.

   B. You must give clear signals and operate with reasonable safety before you may leave a designated bike lane.

BICYCLE PARKING   21210

You may not leave your bicycle on a sidewalk in a way that impedes pedestrian traffic.

FREEWAYS   21960

You must obey signs which indicate freeways or expressways on which bicycle traffic is forbidden.

HAND SIGNALS   21211

It is required for bicyclists to signals turns and sudden changes in speed.

Left turn signal — left hand and arm fully extended and horizontal.

Right turn signal — left hand and arm extended to the left and the forearm pointing upward.

Slowing or stopping — left hand and arm extended downward and the palm open-faced to the rear.

Sierra Azul Open Space Preserve   Photo: Conrad J. Boisvert

BICYCLING TIPS

Benefit from the experience of others by familiarizing yourself with these simple tips for better and safer cycling.

GENERAL RULES OF THE ROAD

1. Always ride on the right and never ride against the flow of traffic. Remember that bicycles are subject to the same driving rules as cars.
2. Keep as far to the right as possible in order to allow cars plenty of room to pass. Always ride in a single file.
3. Signal when turning or slowing down in order to allow the rider behind you to prepare for the same, and to allow cars to know what you are doing. Never act suddenly, except in an absolute emergency.
4. Never ride on freeways. This is simply too dangerous.
5. Cross railroad tracks at right angles to the tracks.
6. Cross cattleguards by getting off and walking your bike.
7. In the rain or on wet surfaces, ride slower and more cautiously than you normally would. Remember that not only are the roads wet, but your brakes are wet as well.
8. Avoid night riding. If you absolutely must, be sure to wear highly visible clothing and carry a light.
9. Never assume that a car or another cyclist will give you the right of way. Always drive defensively.
10. Be extra cautious when passing parked cars. Watch out for doors opening suddenly.
11. Avoid riding on sidewalks.
12. When making a left turn in traffic, ride assertively, but give clear signals. Be sure to wave appreciatively when another vehicle gives you clearance.
13. Always stop at red lights and stop signs. Cyclists have no special privileges.

RULES FOR OFF-ROAD BIKING

1. Know the rules for the area in which you are riding. Always stay on the trails intended for bikes. Leave the area just as you found it.
2. Yield to equestrians. Horses may spook when a bicycle appears suddenly.
3. Yield to hikers. Remember that they had use of the trails first.
4. Always be courteous. Nothing is worse for the sport than ill-will created by impolite actions.
5. Look ahead to anticipate encounters with others.

6. Avoid contact with trailside growth. Poison oak is very common in the South Bay and can be a very unpleasant experience.

7. Carry maps at all times. Getting lost is no fun.

TIPS ON YOUR EQUIPMENT

1. Always carry a spare tire, a tire pump, and tools.

2. Be prepared to fix your own bike. Don't count on others to do this for you.

3. Check your equipment before you go, not after you are underway. Check tire pressure, seat height, brakes, and shifters each time you ride.

4. Tire pressure is usually indicated on the side of the tire. Mountain biking in rough terrain often works better when the tires are deflated a bit. Road riding, on the other hand, requires fully inflated tires for maximum efficiency.

5. Carry an adequate supply of water. This is especially true on hot days or when riding in areas with no services along the way.

6. A handlebar pack or panniers are a convenience for carrying extra clothing or snacks.

7. Equip your bike with reflectors. They don't add much weight and make it easier for others to see you.

8. Toe clips give you better riding efficiency on long rides. Mountain bikes are probably better without them, since quick dismounting may be necessary in rough terrain.

9. A rear view mirror is a useful accessory and will permit you to see approaching riders and vehicles without turning around. This is especially true if you ride with groups and want to keep track of trailing riders.

10. A chain and padlock are recommended if you anticipate leaving your bike unattended and out of view.

APPROPRIATE CLOTHING

1. A helmet is mandatory. Your head is a very important part of your body and is very vulnerable without protection.

2. Wear bright clothing. You want to be easily seen by vehicle drivers.

3. Lycra shorts are not required, but will offer more comfort on long rides. The constant rubbing of loose fitting shorts will be an annoyance and may cause a skin irritation.

4. Gloves are not required, but long rides without them can often cause blisters as well as problems with blood circulation.

5. Bicycling shoes are usually only necessary for competitive riders or for those with surplus cash. Most recreational riders don't really need them. Tennis or running shoes work fine.

6. It is a good idea to carry a lightweight windbreaker, even on warm days. High altitudes or roads along the coast are often colder than you anticipate. Furthermore, if you perspire a lot on an uphill climb, you may want to put on the windbreaker for the downhill.

7. Long pants and winter gloves are usually necessary for rides during the colder months.

8. Some sort of eyewear is strongly recommended. Either cycling goggles or sunglasses will provide protection from dirt, debris, and insects as well as screen your eyes from the harmful effects of the sun's ultraviolet rays.

TECHNIQUES

1. A properly adjusted seat height will ensure your comfort and help avoid knee injuries (quite common to cyclists). The correct seat height should result in a slight bend of the knee when the leg is fully extended to the lower pedal.

2. Be familiar with gear shifting so you can anticipate hill climbs and shift before you need to. It is difficult to shift when there is a lot of pressure on the pedals. Always shift while you are pedaling to ensure that the chain does not derail.

3. Be ready to brake quickly, as hazards can suddenly appear.

4. The upright position (on dropped handlebars) is usually most comfortable for the majority of your riding. Position yourself on the lower bars to reduce your wind resistance on downhill runs.

5. If your bike is equipped with toe clips, try pulling up on the pedals, as well as pushing down. This uses different muscles and can give you better efficiency for the longer rides.

6. When riding a mountain bike on fire trails, it is common to encounter steep downhill sections. To safely deal with these, stop and lower your seat before you do the downhill. This lowers your center of gravity and allows you to dismount quickly without falling to the ground. Raise your seat back to its normal position for uphill sections, to obtain optimum leverage on the pedals.

7. Control your speed, especially on wet road surfaces or on loose gravel of off-road trails. It is very difficult and dangerous to slow down under these conditions.

8. When riding with a group, it is both safe and polite to regroup periodically. Avoid getting spread out over great distances. It is usually best to have an experienced rider follow in the rear of the group to assist any cyclists having problems.

ABOUT THE AUTHOR

Conrad Boisvert was born in Newark, New Jersey, in 1943, and has been a resident of Santa Clara County since 1972. An electronics engineer, he has worked for a variety of high-technology companies over the years. He has always been an avid outdoors-oriented person, with special interests in cycling, tennis, and hiking.

This book is his first, and is a direct result of his interest in recreational cycling and of his desire to share with others the many roads in the South Bay that he has explored on his own. He currently resides in San Jose.